Step - by - Step

PASTA COOKING

Step - by - Step

PASTA COOKING

LESLEY MACKLEY

PHOTOGRAPHED BY

JON STEWART

GREENWICH EDITIONS

Published 1999 by Greenwich Editions,
10 Blenheim Court, Brewery Road, London N7 9NT

A member of the Chrysalis Group plc

ISBN 0 862 88 2710

Managing Editor: Felicity Jackson
Designer: Roger Daniels
Home Economist: Sarah Bush
Photographer: Jon Stewart, assisted by Alister Thorpe
Typeset by AKM Associates (UK) Ltd, Southall, London
Colour separation by J. Film Process Ltd, Bangkok, Thailand
Printed and bound in Spain by Just Colour Graphic, S.L.

ACKNOWLEDGEMENTS
The Publishers would like to thank the following for their help and advice:
The Covent Garden General Store, 107-115 Long Acre, Covent Garden, London WC2 4BA
Elizabeth David Ltd, 46 Bourne Street, London SW1 and at Covent Garden Kitchen Supplies, 3 North Row, The Market, London WC2
Neal Street East, The Oriental specialist, 5 Neal Street, Covent Garden, London WC2

Contents

INTRODUCTION

Pasta is one of the simplest foods, being little more than a flour and water paste, which may be enriched with eggs, yet it is one of the world's favourite foods.

Perfect pasta dishes start with the right pasta, and STEP BY STEP PASTA COOKING begins with a guide to the various types of dried pasta available and how to cook them. There are also recipes for delicious homemade pasta with colourful variations, such as herb and tomato.

The recipes are gathered from all parts of the world and include pasta-based soups and salads, dozens of different casseroles, baked pasta dishes, stuffed pasta and deep-fried pasta, as well as some very unusual and tasty pasta-based desserts and all kinds of sauces to serve with pasta. As well as pasta dishes for those who enjoy meat and seafood, there is a variety of delicious vegetarian dishes.

Temptingly photographed in full colour, STEP BY STEP PASTA COOKING contains an enormous range of dishes to suit all occasions and tastes.

TYPES OF PASTA

There are dozens of different types of pasta and some are more suited to a particular dish than others, but pasta of a similar shape may be substituted in any of the recipes in this book.

The secret of cooking pasta successfully is to use plenty of water. Allow 1.2 litres (2 pints/4¾ cups) for every 125 g (4 oz) pasta. Bring the water to the boil, add 3 teaspoons oil and 3 teaspoons salt to each 500 g (1 lb) pasta. Then add the pasta. Long pasta such as spaghetti should be fanned out slowly into the water as it softens. Bring back to the boil and continue boiling until the pasta is cooked. To test whether it is done, remove a piece from the water and bite into it. It should be *al dente*, or slightly firm. If the pasta is to be cooked again in a baked dish, undercook it slightly, as it will continue to cook in the oven.

Drain the pasta in a colander, shaking to remove most of the water, but leave a little water clinging to it to prevent it from sticking. Pour the pasta into a warmed serving dish and toss with a little olive oil, butter or some of the sauce which accompanies it. If the pasta is to be served in a salad or reheated in a baked dish, it may be rinsed in cold water and drained.

The cooking times for pasta vary according to its size and shape. Follow the directions below as a guideline for dried pasta, but keep testing during the cooking time, to avoid overcooking. Wholewheat pasta takes longer, and fresh pasta much less time to cook than ordinary dried pasta.

Lasagne (1) Cooking time: Some lasagne requires no pre-cooking and is layered straight into a dish with sauce and baked in the oven. Other lasagne must be boiled for 10 minutes before being layered with other ingredients.
Uses: Layered with meat, fish or vegetable sauces. May also be rolled round filling, like cannelloni.

Pappardelle (2) Cooking time: 8 minutes.
Uses: Traditionally served with hare sauce.

Tagliatelle (3) and Fettucine (4) Cooking time: 6 minutes.
Uses: Similar to spaghetti, but particularly good with creamy sauces which adhere better than heavy sauces. May also be fried.

Spaghetti (5) Cooking time: 12 minutes.
Uses: Served simply with butter or oil, or with almost any kind of sauce.

Spaghettini (6) Cooking time: 8 minutes.
Uses: Traditionally served with fish and shellfish sauces. Also good with tomato sauce.

Vermicelli (7) Cooking time: 5 minutes.
Uses: Very thin vermicelli sold in clusters is ideal for serving with very light sauces. Long vermicelli is used in the same way as spaghetti.

Macaroni (8) and Bucatini (9) Cooking time: 8-10 minutes.
Uses: Often used in baked dishes, particularly those with a cheese-based sauce.

Rigatoni (10) Cooking time: 10 minutes.
Uses: Generally used in baked dishes. The ridges help the sauce to cling to the pasta. It may also be stuffed.

Penne (11) Cooking time: 10 minutes.
Uses: Served with meat sauces, which catch in the hollows.

Cannelloni (12) Cooking time: Most cannelloni tubes require no pre-cooking and are stuffed directly before baking. If they are to be fried, they should be boiled first for about 7-10 minutes.
Uses: Filled cannelloni may be baked

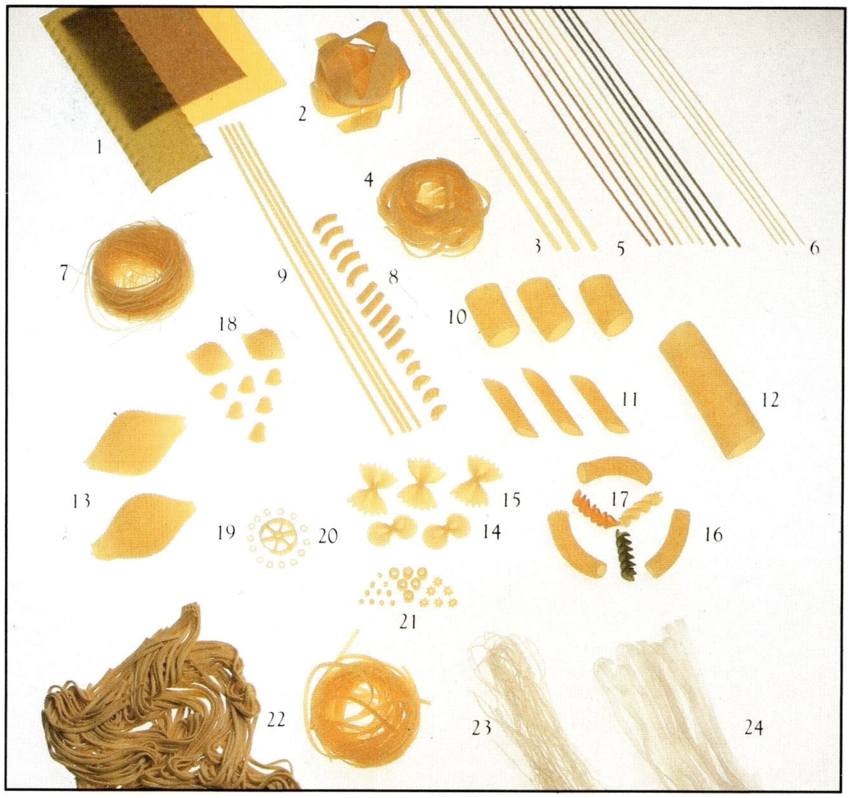

in the oven in a sauce, or topped with butter and grated cheese, and may also be deep-fried until crisp.

Conchiglie (13) Cooking time: Large shells take about 15 minutes to cook and smaller ones 10 minutes.
Uses: Large shells may be stuffed, and their shape makes a fish filling particularly appropriate. Smaller shells are used in casseroles and soup, and served cold in salads.

Fiochetti (bows) (14) and Farfalle (butterflies) (15) Cooking time: 10 minutes.
Uses: Ideal for serving with meat or vegetable sauces, which become trapped in the folds.

Fusilli (16) and Tortiglioni (spirals) (17) Cooking time: 10 minutes.
Uses: Served with substantial meat sauces, which are trapped in the twists. Also good in salads.

Lumache (18) Cooking time: 10 minutes.
Uses: Similar to conchiglie.

Rotini (wheels) (19) and Anelli (20) Cooking time: 8 minutes.
Uses: Added to savoury bakes and salads.

Pastina (anellini, ditalini, stellini) (21) Cooking time: 8 minutes.
Uses: Most often added to soups, but may be used in other dishes.

Egg Noodles (22) Cooking time: 4-5 minutes.
Uses: Flat noodles are often served in soups. Round ones are served in sauces, and are best for stir-frying. Also served as an accompaniment instead of rice.

Rice Noodles (23) Cooking time: Simply soak in hot water for 10-15 minutes.
Uses: Served in spicy sauces, soups and stir-fry dishes.

Transparent (Cellophane) Noodles (24) Cooking time: Soak in hot water for 5 minutes.
Uses: Added to soups or deep-fried as a garnish.

PASTA DOUGH

2 eggs	
185 g (6 oz/1½ cups) strong white bread flour	
pinch of salt	

Any quantity of pasta may be made by using the proportions of 1 egg to 90 g (3 oz/¾ cup) flour, but the most convenient quantity for a beginner to handle is a 2 or 3-egg mixture. Larger amounts should be mixed and rolled in batches.

Beat eggs in a large bowl. Sift flour and salt into bowl. Mix together with a fork, then press with the hands to form a solid piece of dough. It should be firm but pliable, and not sticky. Add more flour if it seems too moist.

Turn dough onto a lightly floured surface and knead firmly for 5-10 minutes until smooth. Wrap in a damp tea towel and leave to rest for 30 minutes at room temperature.

PASTA DOUGH VARIATIONS

PASTA VERDE
Cook 125 g (4 oz) spinach, then drain, squeeze out as much moisture as possible and chop very finely. Add spinach to eggs and flour, adding extra flour if necessary.

TOMATO PASTA
Add 3 teaspoons tomato purée (paste) to the eggs and flour.

HERB PASTA
Add 3 teaspoons of a single chopped fresh herb, such as parsley, or mixed fresh herbs to the eggs and flour.

WHOLEWHEAT PASTA
Use wholewheat bread flour instead of white flour, or for a lighter texture, use a mixture of wholewheat and white flour.

ROLLING DOUGH BY HAND

To roll pasta dough by hand, you need a long rolling pin and a large, clean work surface. It is essential to work quickly or the pasta will dry out and crack. Lightly flour the work surface. Press the dough flat with your hands and roll it out firmly with the rolling pin. Starting from the centre, roll away from you. Keep lifting the sheet of pasta on the rolling pin and turning it 45 degrees. As you roll, lift the far edge on the rolling pin and push it away from you to stretch the dough.

As the sheet of pasta becomes larger, allow it to hang over the edge of the table to increase the stretch. Eventually the sheet of pasta should look smooth and suede-like in texture, and be so thin that you can read newsprint through it!

However, as the sheet of pasta becomes large, it becomes more difficult to turn and unless you are an expert, you will not be able to roll it as thinly by hand as with a machine. In some cases you may find you need a slightly larger quantity of pasta than that given in a recipe.

If making lasagne or filled pasta, such as ravioli or tortellini, the pasta should be used immediately. Otherwise it should be spread out on a tea towel and left to dry for 30 minutes. Turn it over after 15 minutes. Leave to dry enough to prevent it sticking, but not so much that it becomes brittle. The dough is then ready for cutting into shapes.

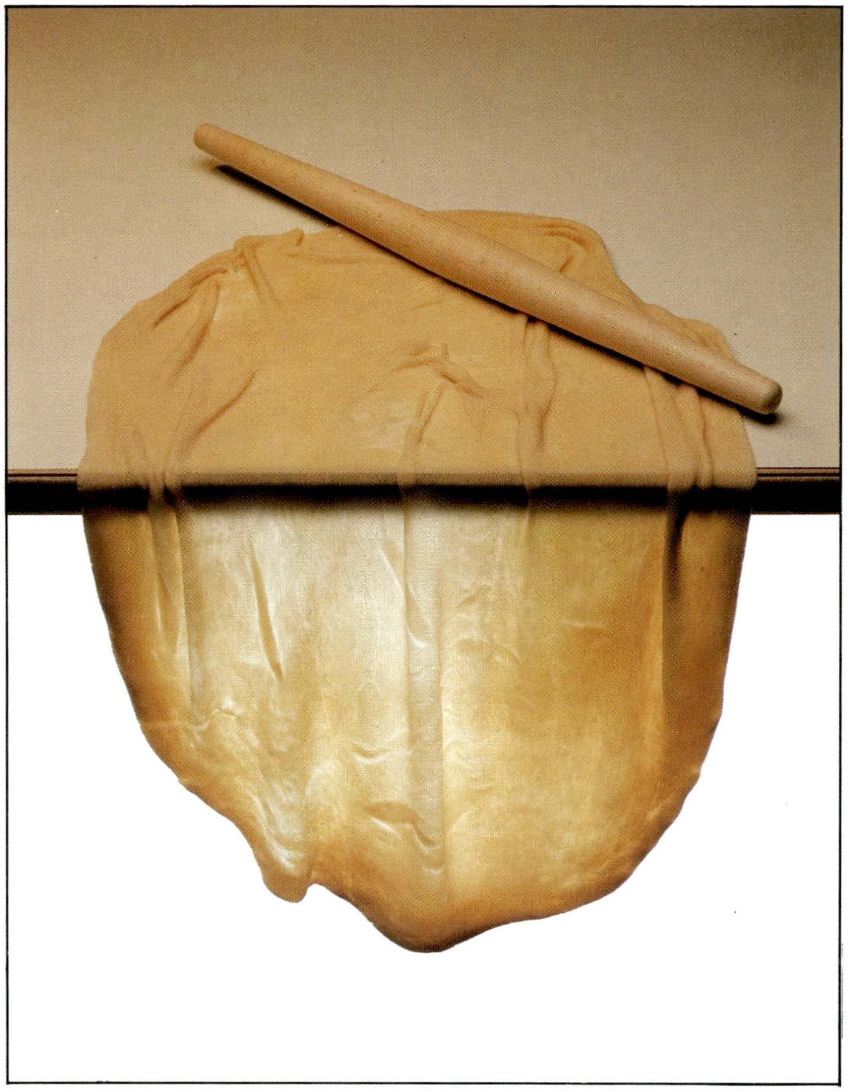

CUTTING PASTA SHAPES

TAGLIATELLE
Loosely roll up the pasta dough into a cylinder. Using a sharp knife, cut the cylinder into even widths. Shake out the coils into loose nests. These may be cooked straight away or left to dry for several days before being stored.

LASAGNE & CANNELLONI
Using a sharp knife or serrated pasta-cutting wheel, cut lasagne sheets to whatever size will best fit your dish. For most purposes, sheets measuring 10 x 12 cm (4 x 5 in) are the most convenient. For cannelloni, cut pasta as for lasagne. The sheets can then be cooked and rolled round a stuffing before baking in the oven.

PAPPARDELLE & FARFALLE
For pappardelle, using a serrated pasta-cutting wheel, cut pasta into strips 2 cm (¾ in) wide and 30 cm (12 in) long. For farfalle, cut pasta sheet into 5 cm (2 in) squares with pasta-cutting wheel. Pinch each square together in the middle to produce a butterfly effect.

Note: Cut pasta trimmings into pretty shapes with a biscuit or aspic cutter. Use for garnishing soups.

PASTA MACHINES

Electric machines are available which mix the dough and then extrude it through a selected cutter to give a variety of shapes, but unless you intend to make large quantities of pasta on a regular basis, a machine is not essential.

The pasta dough can either be made by hand, see page 10, or it can be mixed in a food processor. To make it in a food processor, break the eggs into the bowl and process for 30 seconds, then add the sifted flour and salt and process until the mixture forms a ball.

Rolling pasta in a machine

Rolling pasta dough in a machine is much quicker and easier than rolling it by hand.

The most useful machine is a hand cranking one that rolls the pasta dough into sheets. The space between the rollers is reduced until the dough is thin enough to use, see opposite. The sheets are then passed through cutters of different widths.

Different cutters

By fitting cutters of various sizes onto the pasta rolling machine, it is possible to cut spaghetti or noodles in several different widths.

When cutting spaghetti, it is important not to use very long sheets of pasta, otherwise they tend to stick together. Once the dough is cut into long strands, they need to be left to dry before using. Place a tea towel over the back of a chair and spread out the pasta.Leave to dry for about 30 minutes.

ROLLING DOUGH IN A MACHINE

Divide dough into as many pieces as the number of eggs used. Set the rollers of the machine to the widest setting. Flatten the pieces of dough and roll each piece through the machine.

Fold each piece into 3 crosswise and feed it though again. Repeat about 7 times until the sheet of pasta is smooth and silky. Set rollers one notch closer together and feed pasta through once only. Keep setting rollers closer together and feed pasta through once on each setting.

Cut sheets of pasta in half if they become too long to handle easily. A final rolling on narrowest but one setting should produce pasta of correct thickness for most purposes.

MAKING FILLED PASTA

RAVIOLI

Prepare filling first and set it aside. Make the pasta dough and roll it into strips. Lay the strips out on a tea towel or floured surface. Keep covered with a damp cloth while filling a few at a time.

Place small mounds (about ½ teaspoon) of filling at 4 cm (1½ in) intervals over one sheet of pasta and lay a second sheet over the top.

Press down firmly between the mounds of pasta and cut between the mounds with a pasta-cutting wheel. Spread the ravioli out on a tea towel to dry for about 30 minutes, turning them over after 15 minutes. Take care to keep them separate or they will stick together.

ROUND RAVIOLI

This is made by cutting circles from the filled sheets of pasta, using a sharp knife, serrated pasta-cutting wheel or a special round pasta-cutting stamp.

HALF MOON RAVIOLI

Cut circles about 5 cm (2 in) in diameter. Place a pea-sized amount of filling in the middle. Fold over one side of the circle and press edges firmly together. Leave to dry as for ravioli.

TORTELLINI

Cut circles about 5 cm (2 in) in diameter. Place a pea-sized amount of filling slightly to one side of the middle. Fold over one side of the circle so that it falls just short of the other side. Press edges firmly together. Curve the semi-circle round and pinch edges together. Leave to dry as for ravioli.

CAPPELLETTI

Cut 5 cm (2 in) squares of pasta. Put a small amount of filling in centre of each square. Fold in half diagonally to form a triangle, leaving a slight overlap between edges. Press firmly to seal. Wrap 1 long side of triangle round a finger until the 2 ends overlap. Press ends firmly together, with points of the triangle upright. Leave to dry as for ravioli.

SPINACH SOUP

1 litre (32 fl oz/4 cups) Chicken Stock	
60 g (2 oz/½ cup) anellini	
250 g (8 oz/1 cup) frozen chopped spinach, thawed	
salt and pepper	
2 egg yolks, beaten	

Put chicken stock into a large saucepan. Bring to the boil.

Add anellini and spinach. Cook for 10 minutes, stirring occasionally, until pasta is tender. Season with salt and pepper.

Pour a little hot soup onto egg yolks in a bowl. Stir egg mixture into soup. Do not allow soup to boil. Serve at once.

Serves 4-6.

Variation: Instead of anellini, use off-cuts of pasta cut into attractive shapes with an aspic cutter.

PENANG FISH SOUP

250 g (8 oz) fish trimmings (bones, skins, heads)	
500 g (1 lb) skinned white fish fillets, such as cod or haddock	
1 teaspoon chopped fresh parsley	
salt and pepper	
60 g (2 oz) wide rice noodles or rice sticks	
vegetable oil for deep frying	
finely chopped spring onion and parsley, to garnish	

Put fish trimmings into a saucepan with 940 ml (30 fl oz/3¾ cups) salted water. Bring to the boil, cover pan and simmer gently for 20 minutes.

In a blender or food processor, process fish until it forms a smooth paste. Add parsley. Season with salt and pepper. Roll half the paste into small balls 1 cm (½ in) in diameter. Flatten out remaining paste into a rectangular cake 5 cm (2 in) wide. Cut into strips. In a deep fat fryer, heat oil to 190C (375F) until cube of day-old bread turns golden in 40 seconds. Deep fry strips until crisp and golden. Drain on absorbent kitchen paper. Keep hot.

Strain the fish broth through a fine sieve into a saucepan. Bring back to the boil. Add fishballs. Cook gently for 5 minutes. Meanwhile, in a large saucepan of boiling salted water, cook noodles until just tender. Drain; divide between 4 heated bowls. Divide fishballs between bowls. Pour over broth. Arrange fried fish slices on top. Garnish with chopped spring onion and parsley.

Serves 4.

MINESTRONE SOUP

- 9 teaspoons olive oil
- 4 rashers streaky bacon, cut into matchsticks
- 1 onion, chopped
- 2 carrots, chopped
- 2 sticks celery, chopped
- 250 g (8 oz) white cabbage, roughly shredded
- 1 courgette (zucchini), diced
- 125 g (4 oz) French beans, cut into 2.5 cm (1 in) lengths
- 1.5 litres (2½ pints/6 cups) Chicken Stock
- 440 g (14 oz) can tomatoes
- salt and pepper
- 125 g (4 oz/¾ cup) macaroni
- 3 teaspoons chopped fresh parsley
- freshly grated Parmesan cheese, to serve

In a large saucepan, heat olive oil. Add bacon, onion, carrots and celery. Cook gently until beginning to soften.

Add cabbage, courgette (zucchini), beans, stock and tomatoes and season with salt and pepper. Bring to the boil, cover and simmer for about 2 hours.

Add macaroni. Cook for a further 10-15 minutes until macaroni is tender. Add parsley. Serve with Parmesan cheese handed separately.

Serves 6-8.

Variation: Vary the vegetables according to taste and availability. Soaked haricot beans may be added at the beginning of the cooking time. Pesto, see page *25*, may be stirred in before serving. Add to taste.

WHITE ONION SOUP

- 60 g (2 oz/¼ cup) butter
- 3 onions, finely sliced
- 3 teaspoons plain flour
- 315 ml (10 fl oz/1¼ cups) boiling water
- 940 ml (30 fl oz/3¾ cups) milk
- 60 g (2 oz/⅔ cup) straight vermicelli, broken into 1 cm (½ in) pieces
- salt and pepper
- bacon rolls and sprigs of parsley, to garnish

In a saucepan, melt butter. Add onions. Cook gently until soft.

Stir in flour. Gradually add boiling water. Cook, stirring, until smooth and thickened. Stir in milk.

Bring to the boil. Add vermicelli and season with salt and pepper. Cover pan. Cook, stirring frequently, until vermicelli is tender. Serve in individual bowls, garnished with bacon rolls and sprigs of parsley.

Serves 4-6.

LIGHT VEGETABLE SOUP

940 ml (30 fl oz/3¾ cups) vegetable stock, made from vegetable trimmings or stock cube
2 carrots, peeled
2 sticks celery, thinly sliced
90 g (3 oz) button mushrooms, thinly sliced
60 g (2 oz/¾ cup) frozen peas
30 g (1 oz/2 tablespoons) small pasta shells
salt and pepper
1 tablespoon chopped fresh parsley

Put stock into a saucepan and bring to the boil.

With the pointed end of a potato peeler, cut grooves down carrots. Cut into thin slices. Add to stock with celery, mushrooms, peas and pasta.

Bring to the boil, then cover pan and simmer for about 15 minutes, or until pasta and vegetables are tender. Season with salt and pepper to taste. Pour the soup into individual bowls and sprinkle the chopped parsley over the top of each portion,

Serves 4.

TOMATO & PASTA SOUP

8 tomatoes
60 g (2 oz/¼ cup) butter
1 onion, finely chopped
60 g (2 oz/⅓ cup) ditalini or elbow macaroni
1 litre (32 fl oz/4 cups) Chicken Stock
pinch of saffron powder
pinch of chilli powder
salt
sprigs of parsley, to garnish

Put tomatoes in a bowl. Pour over boiling water. Leave for 1 minute, then drain. Pour over cold water. Leave for 1 minute, then drain. Remove the skins and chop the tomato flesh.

In a saucepan, melt butter. Add onion. Cook until beginning to soften. Add ditalini or macaroni and cook for 2 minutes, stirring.

Add tomatoes, stock and saffron. Bring to boil. Cover and simmer until pasta is tender. Stir in chilli powder and salt to taste. Pour soup into individual bowls and garnish with a sprig of parsley.

Serves 4.

BEAN & PASTA SOUP

6 teaspoons olive oil
1 onion, finely chopped
1 clove garlic, crushed
2 carrots, finely chopped
2 sticks celery, finely chopped
1.5 litres (2½ pints/6 cups) Chicken Stock
salt and pepper
90 g (3 oz/1½ cups) pasta shells
440 g (14 oz) can borlotti beans
celery leaves, to garnish

In a large saucepan, heat oil. Add onion, garlic, carrots and celery and cook gently until soft.

Add chicken stock and season with salt and pepper. Bring to the boil, cover and simmer for 20 minutes. Add pasta and cook for a further 10 minutes, or until pasta is tender.

Drain beans. Rinse in cold water. Sieve half the beans, or process in a blender or food processor. Add puréed and whole beans to soup. Stir well. Cook for 2 minutes to heat through. Serve in individual bowls, garnished with celery leaves.

Serves 6-8.

CHICKEN NOODLE SOUP

1 litre (1¾ pints/4 cups) Chicken Stock
1 carrot, cut into matchsticks
1 leek, thinly sliced
125 g (4 oz) cooked chicken, chopped
90 g (3 oz) round egg noodles
salt and pepper
coriander leaves, to garnish

In a large saucepan, bring stock to the boil. Add carrot and leek. Cover pan and simmer for about 5 minutes, or until carrot and leek are tender.

Stir in chicken and egg noodles and season with salt and pepper. Cook for 5-10 minutes until noodles are tender. Serve at once in individual bowls, garnished with coriander leaves.

Serves 4.

AVGOLEMONO SOUP

1 litre ($1\frac{3}{4}$ pints/4 cups) Chicken Stock	
45 g ($1\frac{1}{2}$ oz/$\frac{1}{3}$ cup) pastini	
salt and pepper	
2 eggs	
juice of 1 lemon	
lemon slices and sprigs of mint, to garnish	

In a saucepan, heat chicken stock. Bring to the boil. Add pastini and season to taste with salt and pepper. Cook for 5 minutes until pastini is tender.

In a bowl, beat eggs. Add lemon juice and beat to mix thoroughly. Pour a ladleful of hot stock onto the beaten eggs, whisking them continuously.

Pour egg mixture into stock in saucepan. Over a very low heat, whisk continuously for 3-4 minutes without boiling until soup thickens slightly. Pour into individual bowls and garnish with lemon slices and sprigs of mint.

Serves 4.

WONTON SOUP

24 filled wonton	
few Chinese leaves, shredded	
1 carrot, cut into strips	
1 spring onion, finely chopped	
CHICKEN STOCK:	
1 boiling fowl with giblets	
1 leek	
1 stick celery	
1 small bunch of parsley	
1 onion	
salt and pepper	

To make stock, put boiling fowl, giblets and 2 litres ($3\frac{1}{2}$ pints/8 cups) water into a large flameproof casserole or saucepan.

Tie together leek, celery and parsley. Add to casserole with onion, salt and pepper. Bring to boil, then cover and simmer for 2 hours, occasionally removing any scum from the surface. Strain stock and adjust seasoning. When cool, refrigerate until required.

Remove fat from surface of stock. In a saucepan, put 940 ml (30 fl oz/$3\frac{3}{4}$ cups) stock. Bring to boil. Drop wonton into stock with the Chinese leaves and carrot strips. Boil rapidly for 2-3 minutes. Spoon into individual bowls and garnish with finely chopped spring onion.

Serves 4-6.

Note: The meat from the boiling fowl can be used in other dishes. The remaining stock will keep for several days in the refrigerator, or may be stored in the freezer.

SMOKED SALMON ROULADE

3 sheets lasagne
1 bunch watercress, washed and trimmed
3 spring onions, very finely chopped
3 teaspoons olive oil
1 teaspoon horseradish sauce
salt and pepper
1 avocado
juice of $\frac{1}{2}$ a lemon
90 g (3 oz) smoked salmon
60 ml (2 fl oz/$\frac{1}{4}$ cup) mayonnaise
60 ml (2 fl oz/$\frac{1}{4}$ cup) crème fraîche
1 tablespoon chopped fresh dill weed
lemon slice and sprig of dill, to garnish

In a large saucepan of boiling salted water, cook pasta until just tender. Drain, rinse in cold water, then pat dry.

In a saucepan of boiling water, blanch watercress for 10 seconds. Drain and refresh in a bowl of cold water. Squeeze gently in a cloth to dry, then chop finely.

In a bowl, mix together watercress, spring onions, olive oil, horseradish sauce, salt and pepper. Peel, halve and stone avocado. Cut into slices lengthwise. Toss in lemon juice.

Spread a little watercress mixture over each sheet of lasagne. Lay a slice of smoked salmon on each sheet. Arrange slices of avocado in a line down the length of the middle of each sheet.

Starting with a long side of pasta, roll up Swiss roll fashion. Wrap each roll in plastic wrap. Chill for 2 hours. In a bowl, mix together mayonnaise, crème fraîche and dill weed, salt and pepper. Add a little milk, if necessary, to make a pouring consistency. Cut each roll diagonally into slices 2 cm/$\frac{3}{4}$ in wide. Garnish with lemon slice and sprig of dill and serve with dill sauce.

Serves 4-6 as a first course.

SEAFOOD PASTA SALAD

375 g (12 oz) monkfish
60 ml (2 fl oz/$\frac{1}{4}$ cup) dry white wine
250 g (8 oz/4 cups) green pasta spirals
90 g (3 oz) smoked salmon trout
125 g (4 oz/$\frac{3}{4}$ cup) peeled prawns
2 teaspoons chopped fresh dill weed
lemon slices and sprigs of dill, to garnish
SALAD DRESSING:
$\frac{1}{2}$ teaspoon Dijon mustard
salt and pepper
1 clove garlic, crushed
3 teaspoons lemon juice
75 ml (2$\frac{1}{2}$ fl oz/$\frac{1}{3}$ cup) olive oil

Cut monkfish into cubes. Put into a saucepan with wine and sufficient water to cover. Cook for a few minutes until fish is tender. Drain, then leave to cool.

In a large saucepan of boiling salted water, cook pasta spirals until tender. Drain and rinse with cold water.

Cut salmon trout into strips. In a bowl, combine monkfish, salmon trout, prawns, pasta and dill weed.

To make dressing, in a bowl mix together mustard, salt, pepper, garlic and lemon juice. Gradually stir in olive oil. Pour dressing over pasta mixture. Mix well. Serve, garnished with lemon and dill.

Serves 4-6.

THREE-WAY PASTA SALAD

6 spring onions,
1 small red pepper (capsicum)
1 small green pepper (capsicum)
1 quantity Salad Dressing
250 g (8 oz/4 cups) red, green and white pasta shells

Chop spring onions finely. Cut peppers (capsicums) into quarters. Remove seeds, cut into small dice. In a bowl, combine spring onions and peppers (capsicums) with salad dressing.

In a large saucepan of boiling salted water, cook pasta until just tender. Drain, rinse in cold water, then drain thoroughly.

In a serving bowl, mix together dressing and pasta shells.

Serves 4-6.

PASTA NIÇOISE

250 g (8 oz/4 cups) wholewheat pasta spirals
6 canned anchovies, drained
30 g (1 oz/2 tablespoons) black olives
220 g (7 oz) can tuna fish
3 teaspoons chopped fresh parsley
3 teaspoons chopped fresh chives or mint
wedges of hard-boiled egg, to garnish
DRESSING:
salt and pepper
1 teaspoon Dijon mustard
1 clove garlic, crushed
3 teaspoons wine vinegar
75 ml (2½ fl oz/⅓ cup) olive oil

In a large saucepan of boiling salted water, cook pasta spirals until just tender. Drain, rinse in cold water, then drain thoroughly.

Cut each anchovy in half lengthwise. Wrap fillets around olives. Drain tuna fish. In a large bowl, combine pasta, flaked tuna fish, olives, parsley and chives or mint.

To make dressing, in a bowl mix together salt, pepper, mustard, garlic and vinegar. Gradually stir in olive oil. Pour dressing over pasta mixture. Mix thoroughly. Garnish with egg.

Serves 4.

CHICKEN TARRAGON SALAD

250 g (8 oz/4 cups) pasta shells	
1.5 kg (3 lb) chicken, cooked	
250 g (8 oz) seedless grapes	
1 tablespoon chopped fresh tarragon	
60 ml (2 fl oz/¼ cup) mayonnaise	
60 ml (2 fl oz/¼ cup) crème fraîche	
salt and pepper	
sprigs of parsley, to garnish	

In a large saucepan of boiling salted water, cook pasta shells until just tender. Drain, rinse in cold water, then drain again thoroughly.

Remove meat from chicken and cut into pieces. In a bowl, mix together pasta, chicken, grapes and tarragon.

In a bowl, mix together mayonnaise and crème fraîche. Season with salt and pepper. Pour over chicken and mix thoroughly. Serve salad at room temperature garnished with a few sprigs of parsley.

Serves 6

AVOCADO PASTA SALAD

250 g (8 oz/4 cups) pasta bows	
1 large avocado	
grated peel and juice of ½ an orange	
salt and pepper	
orange twists and peel, smoked salmon cornets and sprigs of dill, to garnish	

In a large saucepan of boiling salted water, cook pasta bows. Drain, rinse in cold water then drain thoroughly.

Cut avocado in half and remove stone. Scoop out flesh, taking care to scrape all the dark green flesh from the skin. Put avocado, orange peel and juice, salt and pepper into a blender or food processor. Purée until smooth.

In a large bowl, combine avocado purée and pasta. Mix until pasta is coated with avocado purée. Garnish with orange twists and peel, smoked salmon cornets and sprigs of dill.

Serves 6 as an accompaniment to other dishes.

Note: This salad should be served soon after making, otherwise the avocado will discolour.

Variations: Add peeled prawns or chopped smoked salmon to make an elegant first course.

GREEK PASTA SALAD

125 g (4 oz/¾ cup) taramasalata	
125 ml (4 fl oz/½ cup) Greek strained yogurt	
salt and pepper	
250 g (8 oz) green noodles	
60 g (2 oz/½ cup) feta cheese	
60 g (2 oz/½ cup) black olives	
lemon wedges, to garnish	
green or tomato salad and bread, to serve	

In a large bowl, mix together taramasalata and yogurt and season with salt and pepper.

In a large saucepan of boiling salted water, cook noodles until tender. Drain and rinse with cold water. Add to taramasalata mixture. Mix gently until pasta is well coated with dressing.

Cut feta cheese into small dice. Stir cheese and olives into noodles. Serve, garnished with lemon wedges, with a salad and bread.

Serves 4.

CREAMY MUSHROOM SAUCE

90 g (3 oz/⅓ cup) butter	
125 g (4 oz) mushrooms, sliced	
155 ml (5 fl oz/⅔ cup) crème fraîche	
2 egg yolks	
60 g (2 oz/½ cup) grated Parmesan cheese	
salt and pepper	
pinch of freshly grated nutmeg	
125 g (4 oz/1 cup) frozen peas, thawed	
sprig of mint, to garnish	

In a frying pan, melt 30 g (1 oz/6 teaspoons) butter. Add mushrooms and cook gently until tender. Set aside. In a bowl, beat together crème fraîche, egg yolks, Parmesan cheese, salt, pepper and nutmeg until well combined.

In a saucepan, melt remaining butter. Stir in crème fraîche mixture. Add peas and mushrooms. Over a very low heat, cook gently, stirring, until mixture is heated through and beginning to thicken slightly. Serve at once over pasta, garnished with a sprig of mint.

Serves 4.

MASCARPONE SAUCE

- 15 g (½ oz/3 teaspoons) butter
- 250 g (8 oz/1 cup) mascarpone
- milk (see recipe)
- 90 g (3 oz/¾ cup) walnuts, coarsely chopped
- 30 g (1 oz/¼ cup) grated Parmesan cheese
- salt and pepper

In a saucepan, melt butter. Gradually stir in mascarpone.

Heat gently, stirring until sauce is smooth. Add a little milk if necessary, to give a smooth, creamy consistency.

Stir in walnuts and Parmesan cheese. Season with salt and pepper. Serve at once with spaghetti or tagliatelle.

Serves 4.

CHICKEN LIVER SAUCE

- 30 g (1 oz/6 teaspoons) butter
- 4 rashers bacon, rinds removed, chopped
- 1 onion, finely chopped
- 1 clove garlic, crushed
- 375 g (12 oz) chicken livers, chopped
- 2 teaspoons plain flour
- 185 ml (6 fl oz/¾ cup) Chicken Stock
- 1 teaspoon tomato purée (paste)
- salt and pepper
- 1 teaspoon chopped fresh marjoram
- 60 ml (2 fl oz/¼ cup) thick sour cream
- sprigs of marjoram, to garnish

In a saucepan, melt butter. Add bacon, onion and garlic. Cook until onion is soft.

Stir in chicken livers. Cook, stirring, until livers are no longer pink. Stir in flour.

Gradually stir in the chicken stock. Add tomato purée (paste), salt, pepper and marjoram. Cover. Cook gently for 10 minutes. Stir in cream. Serve in a sauceboat, garnished with sprigs of marjoram, or poured over pasta, such as rigatoni.

Serves 4.

HARE SAUCE

- saddle of hare, weighing about 500 g (1 lb)
- 6 teaspoons vegetable oil
- 6 rashers bacon, rinds removed, chopped
- 1 onion, finely chopped
- 1 carrot, finely chopped
- 2 teaspoons plain flour
- 155 ml (5 fl oz/$^2/_3$ cup) meat stock
- salt and pepper
- freshly grated nutmeg

MARINADE:

- 250 ml (8 fl oz/1 cup) red wine
- 1 onion, sliced
- 1 stick celery, sliced
- 1 bay leaf
- 2 black peppercorns

Put hare into a bowl. Mix together marinade ingredients and pour over hare. Cover bowl. Leave to marinate, in a cool place, for 1-2 days.

In a saucepan, heat oil. Add bacon, onion and carrot. Cook gently until onion is soft. Remove hare from marinade, add to pan and brown all over. Stir in flour. Strain marinade; gradually add to pan with stock. Season with salt, pepper and nutmeg.

Cover pan and cook over a gentle heat for 1½ hours, or until hare is very tender. Remove hare from pan. Cut all meat off the bones and cut into small pieces. Return meat to pan and stir into sauce.

Serves 4.

Note: This sauce is traditionally served with pappardelle, wide ribbon pasta. Garnish with bay leaves.

SHELLFISH SAUCE

- 60 ml (2 fl oz/¼ cup) olive oil
- 500 g (1 lb) fresh mussels in shells, cleaned
- 1 clove garlic, crushed
- 2 shallots, finely chopped
- 185 ml (6 fl oz/$^2/_3$ cup) dry white wine
- salt and pepper
- 250 g (8 oz) can clams
- 6 teaspoons chopped fresh parsley

In a large saucepan, heat half the olive oil. Add mussels. Cover and cook for about 4 minutes until all mussels are open.

Heat remaining oil in pan. Add garlic and shallots. Cook until shallots are soft. Drain mussels. Strain cooking liquid; add to shallots with white wine. Season with salt and pepper. Bring to the boil. Boil gently, uncovered, until reduced slightly.

Remove most mussels from shells leaving a few for garnishing. Drain clams. Add mussels and clams to cooking juice. Sprinkle parsley over. Serve at once.

Serves 4.

CARBONARA SAUCE

30 g (1 oz/6 teaspoons) butter
8 rashers bacon, rinds removed, cut into matchsticks
4 eggs
60 g (2 oz/½ cup) grated Parmesan cheese
6 teaspoons single (light) cream
salt and pepper
3 teaspoons chopped fresh chives

In a saucepan, melt butter. Add bacon. Fry gently until cooked.

In a bowl, beat together eggs, Parmesan cheese and cream and season with salt and pepper. Pour onto bacon. Cook gently, stirring, until eggs are just beginning to thicken.

Stir in chives. Pour sauce over hot pasta, such as spaghetti or tagliatelle. Serve at once.

Serves 4.

PRAWN & GARLIC SAUCE

6 teaspoons olive oil
90 g (3 oz/⅓ cup) butter
2 cloves garlic, finely chopped
250 g (8 oz) peeled prawns
salt and pepper
6 teaspoons chopped fresh chives

In a saucepan, heat oil and butter until butter is melted.

Add garlic and cook gently for 2-3 minutes, stirring occasionally. Stir in prawns. Cook gently until heated through.

Season with salt and pepper. Stir in chopped chives, then pour sauce over hot pasta.

Serves 4.

SALMON & CREAM SAUCE

- 30 g (1 oz/6 teaspoons) butter
- 500 ml (16 fl oz/2 cups) double (thick) cream
- 30 g (1 oz/¼ cup) grated Parmesan cheese
- 250 g (8 oz/2 cups) cooked, flaked salmon
- 3 teaspoons chopped fresh dill
- salt and pepper
- pinch of freshly grated nutmeg
- sprig of dill, to garnish

In a saucepan, heat butter and cream. Bring to just below boiling point.

Simmer gently for about 10 minutes, until thickened and slightly reduced. Add Parmesan cheese.

Stir in salmon, dill, salt, pepper and nutmeg. Serve, garnished with a sprig of dill, with spinach linguini or other thin noodles.

Serves 4 as a first course.

PESTO

- 60 g (2 oz) basil leaves
- 60 g (2 oz/½ cup) pine kernels
- 2 cloves garlic
- salt
- 60 g (2 oz/½ cup) grated Parmesan cheese
- 125 ml (4 fl oz/½ cup) olive oil

Put basil, pine kernels, garlic and salt into a blender or food processor. Process until mixture forms a smooth paste.

Add grated Parmesan cheese to basil mixture in blender or food processor, then process until well blended.

Gradually add olive oil, a little at a time, until sauce has a creamy consistency.

Serves 4-6.

Note: Pesto is used as a sauce for pasta, and is also added to dishes such as minestrone soup to give added flavour.

Variation: When fresh basil is unavailable, a version of pesto may be made with parsley, and walnuts may be used instead of pine kernels.

LEMON PEPPER SAUCE

30 g (1 oz/6 teaspoons) butter
155 ml (5 fl oz/⅔ cup) single (light) cream
1-2 teaspoons green peppercorns
grated peel of 1 lemon
salt

In a saucepan, melt butter. Stir in cream.

Lightly crush peppercorns with the back of a spoon. Add to cream. Stir in lemon peel and salt.

Heat gently, without boiling, until slightly thickened. Combine with cooked pasta and serve.

Serves 4.

Note: This sauce is ideal for serving with fine capellini.

TOMATO SAUCE

500 g (1 lb) tomatoes
4 teaspoons olive oil
1 onion, finely chopped
1 clove garlic, crushed
3 teaspoons tomato purée (paste)
½ teaspoon sugar
3 teaspoons chopped fresh basil
salt and pepper

Put tomatoes in a bowl. Pour over boiling water to cover. Leave for 1 minute. Drain. Peel and chop roughly.

In a saucepan, heat oil. Add onion and garlic. Cook until soft. Stir in chopped tomatoes, tomato purée (paste), sugar, basil, salt and pepper.

Cover pan, simmer gently for about 30 minutes. If a thicker sauce is required, simmer, uncovered, for a few more minutes. Serve with all types of pasta.

Serves 4.

Spaghetti with Meatballs

1 slice bread, crusts removed	
1 onion, very finely chopped	
1 clove garlic, crushed	
500 g (1 lb) ground beef	
3 teaspoons chopped fresh parsley	
salt and pepper	
3 teaspoons vegetable oil	
1 quantity Tomato Sauce	
375 g (12 oz) spaghetti	
60 g (2 oz/½ cup) grated Parmesan cheese	
sprigs of basil, to garnish	

Soak bread in a little water. Squeeze dry and crumble into a bowl. Add onion, garlic, beef and parsley, salt and pepper. Mix well. Shape into 2.5 cm (1 in) balls. In a frying pan, heat oil. Add meatballs and cook for 10 minutes until brown all over. Add tomato sauce and heat through.

Meanwhile, cook spaghetti until tender. Drain well and pour into a heated serving dish. Pour over meatballs and sauce. Sprinkle with Parmesan cheese, garnish with sprigs of basil and serve.

Serves 4.

RICOTTA & HAM SAUCE

30 g (1 oz/6 teaspoons) butter	
2 leeks, finely sliced	
1 clove garlic, crushed	
125g (4 oz) ham	
250 g (8 oz/2 cups) Ricotta cheese	
155 ml (5 fl oz/⅔ cup) thick sour cream	
milk	
pepper	

In a saucepan, melt butter; add sliced leeks and garlic. Cook until leeks are soft.

Cut ham into small squares. Stir into leeks. Cook for a few minutes.

In a bowl, mix together Ricotta and sour cream. Add a little milk, if necessary, to make a smooth creamy sauce. Season with pepper. Add to pan with leeks and ham. Cook gently until sauce is heated through. Serve at once with tagliatelle.

Serves 4.

BÉCHAMEL SAUCE

315 ml (10 fl oz/1¼ cups) milk
½ bay leaf
60 g (2 oz/6 teaspoons) butter
60 g (2 oz/½ cup) plain flour
salt and pepper

In a small saucepan, heat the milk and bay leaf to just below boiling point. Remove from heat. Remove bay leaf.

In a heavy saucepan, melt butter. Stir in flour and cook for 2 minutes, stirring, over gentle heat. Remove from heat.

Gradually stir in milk. Return pan to heat. Stir until thick and smooth. Simmer gently for 10 minutes. Season with salt and pepper. If sauce is not to be used immediately, cover surface closely with plastic wrap.

Serves 4.

Variation: For Ham & Mushroom Sauce, put 185g (6 oz) sliced mushrooms and 9 teaspoons dry cider into a saucepan, cover and cook gently for 5 minutes. Add to Béchamel Sauce made with 440 ml (14 fl oz/1¾ cups) milk and 45 g (1½ oz/9 teaspoons) each butter and plain flour. Stir in 125 g (4 oz) shredded ham and grated nutmeg to taste. Serve with pasta.

GREEN & BLUE SAUCE

250 g (8 oz) broccoli
185 g (6 oz) Gorgonzola cheese
100 g (3½ oz/½ cup) mascarpone
155 ml (5 fl oz/⅔ cup) natural yogurt
pepper

Wash and trim broccoli, discarding stalks. Cut into small flowerets. Cook in boiling salted water for 2-3 minutes until just tender. Drain thoroughly.

Roughly chop Gorgonzola cheese. In a small saucepan, put Gorgonzola and mascarpone. Heat gently, stirring, until Gorgonzola has melted.

Add broccoli and yogurt to cheese sauce. Season with pepper. Heat gently for 2 minutes, stirring occasionally. Pour over pasta.

Serves 4.

MEDITERRANEAN SAUCE

1 aubergine (eggplant)
salt
4 tablespoons olive oil
1 onion, chopped
1 clove garlic, crushed
1 small green pepper (capsicum), seeded
1 small red pepper (capsicum), seeded
1 small yellow pepper (capsicum), seeded
4 tomatoes, peeled and roughly chopped
salt and pepper
½ teaspoon dried oregano

Cut aubergine (eggplant) into strips, put into a colander and sprinkle with salt. Leave for 1 hour.

Pat aubergine slices dry with absorbent kitchen paper.

In a large frying pan, heat oil. Add onion and garlic. Cook gently until soft. Add aubergine (eggplant) strips. Cook for 5 minutes, stirring.

Cut peppers (capsicums) into strips, add to pan and cook for 5 minutes. Stir in tomatoes, salt, pepper and oregano. Cover pan and cook gently for 20 minutes. Serve with spaghetti.

Serves 4.

BOLOGNESE SAUCE

2 tablespoons vegetable oil
60 g (2 oz) rashers bacon, rinds removed, chopped
1 onion, finely chopped
1 carrot, finely chopped
1 stick celery, finely chopped
1 clove garlic, crushed
250 g (8 oz) ground beef
125 g (4 oz) chicken livers, chopped
6 teaspoons tomato purée (paste)
125 ml (4 fl oz/½ cup) dry white wine
125 ml (4 fl oz/½ cup) stock
salt and pepper
pinch of freshly grated nutmeg
celery leaves, to garnish

In a large heavy saucepan, heat oil. Add bacon and cook gently until fat begins to run from the bacon, stirring frequently.

Add onion, carrot, celery and garlic to pan. Cook, stirring, until beginning to brown. Add ground beef and cook, stirring, until evenly browned. Stir in chicken livers and cook for a few minutes, stirring frequently, until they are no longer pink.

Stir in tomato purée (paste), wine and stock and season with salt and pepper and nutmeg. Cover pan and cook gently for 30-40 minutes. Garnish with celery leaves and serve with spaghetti.

Serves 4-6.

CANNELLONI AU GRATIN

- 60 g (2 oz/$^1/_4$ cup) butter
- 1 onion, finely chopped
- 1 clove garlic, crushed
- 375 g (12 oz) mushrooms, sliced
- 3 teaspoons plain flour
- 185 ml (6 fl oz/$^3/_4$ cup) crème fraîche
- salt and pepper
- pinch of freshly grated nutmeg
- 1-egg quantity Herb Pasta
- 6 very thin slices prosciutto
- 30 g (1 oz/$^1/_2$ cup) fresh breadcrumbs
- 30 g (1 oz/$^1/_4$ cup) grated Parmesan cheese
- slices of prosciutto and sprigs of mint, to garnish

In a saucepan, melt the butter. Add onion and garlic and cook until soft. Add mushrooms and cook, stirring, until soft and most of the liquid has evaporated.

Stir in flour, then add 75 ml (2$^1/_2$ fl oz/$^1/_3$ cup) crème fraîche to form a thick sauce. Season with salt, pepper and nutmeg.

Preheat oven to 180C (350F/Gas 4). Grease an ovenproof dish. Roll out pasta, see page 10, and cut 6 rectangles 12.5 x 10 cm (5 x 4 in). Put a slice of prosciutto on each rectangle, lay some mushroom filling across each one and roll up from the short end.

Pack tightly, seams down, in the dish. Pour remaining crème fraîche over and scatter with mixed breadcrumbs and Parmesan. Bake in oven for 20 minutes or until golden and bubbling. Serve at once, garnished with slices of prosciutto and sprigs of mint.

Serves 6 as a first course.

SPINACH CANNELLONI

- 500 g (1 lb) fresh spinach, trimmed and washed
- 30 g (1 oz/6 teaspoons) butter
- 1 onion, finely chopped
- 3 teaspoons plain flour
- 155 ml (5 fl oz/$^2/_3$ cup) milk
- 125 g (4 oz/$^1/_2$ cup) ham, finely chopped
- salt and pepper
- pinch of freshly grated nutmeg
- 8 ready-to-use cannelloni tubes
- 1 quantity Béchamel sauce
- 90 g (3 oz $^3/_4$ cup) grated Cheddar cheese.
- slices of ham and bay leaves, to garnish

In a large saucepan, cook spinach in a little water until tender. Drain spinach and chop finely.

In a saucepan, melt butter, add onion and cook until soft. Stir in flour and cook for 1 minute. Gradually add milk and bring to the boil for 1 minute. Stir in spinach and ham. Season with salt, pepper and nutmeg. Push spinach mixture into cannelloni tubes using a teaspoon.

Preheat oven to 220C (425F/Gas 7). In a saucepan, gently heat white sauce. Stir in 60 g (2 oz/$^1/_2$ cup) cheese. Pour half the sauce into an ovenproof dish. Arrange cannelloni in dish and pour over remaining sauce, arrange ham in a lattice pattern and sprinkle remaining cheese on top. Bake in the oven for 40 minutes until golden and bubbling. Serve, garnished with bay leaves.

Serves 4.

LOBSTER SHELLS

8 conchiglie (large shells)
meat from a 500 g (1 lb) cooked lobster
2 teaspoons lemon juice
salt
cayenne pepper
155 ml (5 fl oz/⅔ cup) double (heavy) cream
½ teaspoon grated lemon peel
2 teaspoons chopped fresh dill
pepper
lemon twist and sprigs of dill, to garnish

In a large saucepan of boiling salted water, cook shells, until just tender. Drain.

Preheat oven to 190C (375F/Gas 5). Chop lobster meat roughly. Put into a bowl with lemon juice, salt, cayenne pepper and 6 teaspoons cream. Mix well together. Fill shells with lobster mixture. Arrange in an ovenproof dish.

In a bowl, mix together remaining cream, lemon peel and dill. Season with salt and pepper. Pour over shells. Cover dish with foil. Bake in the oven for 15-20 minutes until heated through. Baste with sauce halfway through cooking time.

Garnish with a lemon twist and sprigs of dill. Serve at once.

Serves 4 as a first course.

FISH RAVIOLI

250 g (8 oz) white fish fillets, such as cod, cooked and flaked
2 canned anchovies, drained and pounded
30 g (1 oz/¼ cup) grated Parmesan cheese
grated peel and juice of ½ a lemon
1 egg yolk
pepper
freshly grated nutmeg
3-egg quantity Pasta Dough
chopped fresh parsley, blanched shredded leek and strips of lemon peel, to garnish

LEEK SAUCE:
60 g (2 oz/¼ cup) butter
500 g (1 lb) leeks, cleaned and sliced
155 ml (5 fl oz/⅔ cup) fish or Chicken Stock
155 ml (5 fl oz/⅔ cup) thick sour cream.

In a bowl, mix the fish, anchovies, Parmesan cheese, lemon peel and juice and egg yolk. Season with pepper and nutmeg. Process in a blender or food processor until fairly smooth. Roll out pasta dough and, using fish purée as a filling, make ravioli.

While ravioli is drying, make sauce. Melt butter in a saucepan, add leeks and stir round until coated with butter. Cover pan and cook gently until leeks are soft. Add stock, then process in a blender or food processor until smooth. Stir in sour cream. Cook ravioli in boiling water for 8-10 minutes. Meanwhile, warm sauce. Drain ravioli and turn into a warmed serving dish. Pour over sauce. Serve, garnished with parsley, leek and lemon peel.

Serves 6 as a first course.

PASTA & RICOTTA

- 500 g (1 lb) spinach, washed and trimmed
- 250 g (8 oz/2 cups) Ricotta cheese
- 60 g (2 oz/½ cup) grated Parmesan cheese
- 1 egg yolk
- salt and pepper
- freshly grated nutmeg
- 3-egg quantity Pasta Dough
- 90 g (3 oz/⅓ cup) butter
- 5 teaspoons chopped fresh mixed herbs
- 2 teaspoons lemon juice

In a large saucepan, cook spinach in a small amount of water until tender. Drain and leave to cool.

Squeeze spinach dry, then chop in a blender or food processor. Add Ricotta, Parmesan cheese and egg yolk and season with salt, pepper and nutmeg. Process until fairly smooth. Roll out the pasta, see page 10. Cut into 5 cm (2 in) squares. Put ½ teaspoon of filling in middle of each square. Fold in half to make a triangle; press edges to seal. Wrap long side of triangle around index finger; press ends together. Leave on a tea towel to dry, turning after 1 hour.

Cook pasta in a large pan of boiling water for 10-15 minutes. In a small saucepan, melt butter. Stir in herbs and lemon juice. Drain pasta and put into a warmed serving dish. Pour herb butter over and stir thoroughly. Serve at once.

Serves 4 as a main course or 6 as a first course.

Variation: If you have left over Pasta Verde or Tomato Pasta, see page 9, make a mixture of different coloured shapes. If preferred, cut pasta into 5 cm (2 in) circles instead of squares to make this dish.

RAVIOLI WITH SAGE

- 90 g (3 oz/⅓ cup) butter
- 1 onion, peeled and chopped
- 250 g (8 oz) minced pork
- 250 g (8 oz) minced veal
- 2 tablespoons tomato purée (paste)
- salt and pepper
- freshly grated nutmeg
- 30 g (1 oz/½ cup) breadcrumbs
- 2 egg yolks
- 125 g (4 oz/1 cup) grated Parmesan cheese
- 3-egg quantity Pasta Dough
- fresh sage leaves

To make filling, in a saucepan, melt 30 g (1 oz/6 teaspoons) butter, add onion and cook until soft.

Add minced meats and cook, stirring, until brown. Blend tomato purée (paste) with 4 tablespoons water, then stir into pan. Season with salt, pepper and nutmeg to taste. Cover and cook gently for 30 minutes. Leave to cool, then put into a blender or food processor with the breadcrumbs, egg yolks and cheese and process until smooth. Make ravioli, see page 12, filling with meat mixture.

Drop ravioli in boiling salted water and cook for 15-20 minutes. Drain and place in a warmed serving dish. Melt remaining butter and pour over ravioli. Season with pepper and garnish with sage leaves. Serve at once.

Serves 6 as a first course.

TORTELLINI & TOMATO

315 g (10 oz) cooked chicken
125 g (4 oz/½ cup) mortadella
2 eggs
60 g (2 oz/½ cup) grated Parmesan cheese
salt and pepper
freshly grated nutmeg
3-egg quantity Pasta Dough
1 quantity Tomato Sauce
Parmesan cheese for sprinkling

In a blender or food processor, finely chop chicken and mortadella. Add eggs and Parmesan cheese. Season with salt, pepper and nutmeg, then process until fairly smooth.

Roll out pasta, see page 10. Using a plain biscuit cutter, cut out rounds 4 cm (1½ in) in diameter. Put ½ teaspoon of filling in the middle of each round, see page 12.

Fold each round in half over the stuffing so that the upper edge comes just short of the lower edge. Press edges to seal. Curl round index finger, pressing the two points firmly together. Leave on a tea towel to dry, turning after 1 hour.

Cook tortellini in a large saucepan of boiling salted water for about 10 minutes. Meanwhile, in a saucepan, heat tomato sauce. Drain tortellini, tip into a warmed serving dish, pour sauce over, sprinkle with Parmesan cheese and serve.

Serves 4 as a main course or 6 as a first course.

VERMICELLI FLAN

30 g (1 oz/6 teaspoons) butter
2 small leeks, sliced
6 rashers bacon, rinds removed, chopped
125 g (4 oz) fine vermicelli
60 g (2 oz/½ cup) grated Cheddar cheese
155 ml (5 fl oz/⅔ cup) natural yogurt
155 ml (5 fl oz/⅔ cup) single (light) cream
2 eggs, beaten
salt and pepper
1 tomato, sliced
leek leaves, to garnish

In a frying pan, heat butter. Add leeks and bacon. Cook gently until leeks are tender.

Preheat oven to 190C (375F/Gas 5). Grease a 22.5 cm (9 in) flan tin. Meanwhile, in a large saucepan of boiling salted water, cook vermicelli until tender. Drain, return to pan. Stir in cheese. Press vermicelli into the base and sides of flan tin.

Spread bacon and leeks over pasta flan case. In a bowl, beat together yogurt, cream, eggs, salt and pepper. Pour over bacon and leeks. Arrange tomato slices on top. Bake in the oven for 30 minutes or until puffed up and golden brown. Remove flan ring and serve warm or cold, garnished with leek leaves.

Serves 6.

FOUR CHEESE BUCATINI

185 g (6 oz) bucatini
315 ml (10 fl oz/1¼ cups) single (light) cream
60 g (2 oz/½ cup) grated Parmesan cheese
90 g (3 oz) Gruyère cheese, diced
90 g (3 oz/¾ cup) soft goat's cheese
90 g (3 oz) Mozzarella cheese, diced
pepper
chopped Parma ham and chives, to garnish

In a large saucepan of boiling salted water, cook bucatini until tender.

Meanwhile, put cream into a large saucepan with half the Parmesan cheese. Add Gruyère, goat's cheese and Mozzarella. Heat gently until cheeses are melting. Season with pepper.

Drain bucatini. Add to cheese mixture. Stir well. Sprinkle with remaining Parmesan cheese, the Parma ham and chives. Serve at once.

Serves 4.

LASAGNE

250 g (8 oz) lasagne
1 quantity Béchamel Sauce
125 g (4 oz) Mozzarella cheese, cubed
1 quantity Bolognese Sauce
6 teaspoons grated Parmesan cheese

In a large saucepan of boiling salted water, cook lasagne, in two batches, for about 10 minutes until just tender. Drain thoroughly. Spread out on a tea towel.

Preheat the oven to 180C (350F/Gas 4). Grease a rectangular ovenproof dish. In a saucepan, heat Béchamel sauce. Add Mozzarella cheese and stir until melted.

Arrange a layer of lasagne over base of dish. Spoon over half the meat sauce. Cover with lasagne. Spread with half the cheese sauce. Repeat the layers finishing with remaining cheese sauce. Sprinkle Parmesan cheese over top. Bake in the oven for 30-40 minutes.

Serves 4-6.

Note: This dish may be prepared in advance and baked when required. Serve with a salad.

SPINACH PASTA ROLL

- 3 teaspoons vegetable oil
- 1 onion, finely chopped
- 500 g (1 lb) frozen spinach, thawed and drained
- 125 g (4 oz/⅔ cup) cottage cheese
- 125 g (4 oz/1 cup) grated Parmesan cheese
- 1 egg yolk
- salt and pepper
- 1 quantity Pasta Dough
- 60 g (2 oz/¼ cup) butter
- sprigs of watercress, to garnish

In a frying pan, heat oil. Add onion and cook until soft. Add spinach and cook for 2 minutes, stirring frequently.

In a bowl, mix together cottage cheese, half the Parmesan cheese and egg yolk. Season with salt and pepper. Stir in spinach and onion. Roll out pasta dough to a rectangle 30 x 35 cm (12 × 14 in), joining two sheets of pasta together if necessary and moistening the seam with water. Spread with spinach mixture, leaving a border around edge.

Roll up from long edge. Cut in half to make 2 rolls.

Wrap each roll in greaseproof paper, then foil, leaving seam at top. Turn up end of foil to form 'handles'.

Put sufficient water in a pan to come halfway up rolls. Bring to boil, cover and simmer rolls for 30 minutes. Remove from pan, unwrap and leave to cool. Preheat oven to 190C (375F/Gas 5). Cut rolls into 2 cm (¾ in) slices. Arrange in baking dish. Melt butter and pour over slices. Sprinkle with remaining Parmesan. Bake in the oven for 15 minutes until golden. Serve, garnished with sprigs of watercress.

Serves 4.

FISH & PASTA RING

- 185 g (6 oz) tagliatelle verde
- 30 g (1 oz/6 teaspoons) butter
- 4 eggs, beaten
- 315 ml (10 fl oz/1¼ cups) milk
- salt and pepper
- freshly grated nutmeg
- 500 g (1 lb) white fish fillets, such as cod
- 1 quantity Tomato Sauce
- bay leaves, to garnish

In a large saucepan of boiling salted water, cook tagliatelle until tender. Meanwhile, preheat oven to 180C (350F/Gas 4).

In a small saucepan, melt butter. Brush a ring mould generously with melted butter. In a bowl, beat together eggs, milk and remaining butter. Season with salt, pepper and nutmeg. Pour mixture into ring mould. Drain tagliatelle, spoon into ring mould and arrange evenly. Bake in oven for 40 minutes until set.

Meanwhile, skin fish and cut into cubes. Put tomato sauce into a saucepan. Bring to the boil, then add fish. Simmer gently, uncovered, for 10-15 minutes, or until fish is cooked.

Turn out pasta ring onto a large warmed serving dish. Spoon some fish sauce into the centre, pour a little over top of pasta ring and arrange remaining fish and sauce round the edge. Garnish with bay leaves and serve at once.

Serves 4.

— COURGETTE PASTA MOULD —

3 medium courgettes (zucchini), thinly sliced
125 g (4 oz/$2\frac{1}{4}$ cups) wholewheat pasta wheat ears
6 teaspoons vegetable oil
1 large onion, finely chopped
4 tomatoes, peeled and chopped
3 teaspoons tomato purée (paste)
2 teaspoons chopped fresh oregano
1 egg, beaten
salt and pepper
30 g (1 oz/6 teaspoons) butter
radicchio and endive leaves, to serve

In a saucepan of boiling water, cook courgettes (zucchini) for 3-4 minutes until just tender. Drain, then rinse with cold water. Spread out on a tea towel.

In a large pan of boiling salted water, cook wheat ears until just tender. Drain. Meanwhile, heat oil in a frying pan. Add onion and cook gently until soft. In a bowl, mix together pasta, onion, tomatoes, tomato purée (paste), oregano and egg. Season to taste with salt and pepper.

Preheat oven to 200C (400F/Gas 6). Thoroughly butter a ring mould, then line with courgette (zucchini) slices, overlapping them like tiles on a roof.

Fill mould with pasta mixture. Cover with overlapping courgette (zucchini) slices. Dot top with butter. Cover with foil. Bake in the oven for 40 minutes. Turn out onto a serving plate. Serve hot or cold with radicchio and endive leaves.

Serves 6.

—— SMOKED FISH LASAGNE ——

500 g (1 lb) smoked fish fillets, such as haddock
625 ml (20 fl oz/$2\frac{1}{2}$ cups) milk
4 carrots, cut into small dice
4 sticks celery, cut into small dice
90 g (3 oz/$\frac{1}{2}$ cup) butter
6 sheets lasagne verde
3 teaspoons chopped fresh parsley
salt and pepper
60 g (2 oz/$\frac{1}{2}$ cup) plain flour
freshly grated nutmeg
30 g (1 oz/6 teaspoons) grated Parmesan cheese
lime twist and sprig of parsley, to garnish

Put fish and milk into a large saucepan. Bring to the boil, then simmer gently until fish is cooked.

Put carrots and celery into a saucepan with 30 g (1 oz/6 teaspoons) butter and 500 ml (16 fl oz/2 cups) water. Bring to the boil, then simmer until vegetables are tender. Meanwhile, in a large pan of boiling salted water, cook lasagne until just tender. Drain and spread out on a tea towel. Drain fish, reserving cooking liquid, and flake into a bowl. Drain vegetables, reserving liquid, and add to fish with parsley. Season with salt and pepper.

Preheat oven to 190C (375F/Gas 5). Make a Béchamel sauce, see page 28, with remaining butter, flour, vegetable water and milk from fish. Season with salt, pepper and nutmeg. Arrange a layer of lasagne in the base of an ovenproof dish. Cover with one-third of fish mixture then one-third of sauce. Repeat layers twice, ending with sauce. Sprinkle with Parmesan cheese. Bake in the oven for 25 minutes. Serve, garnished with lime twist and parsley.

Serves 4-6.

SMOKED FISH MOUSSE

60 g (2 oz/1 cup) small pasta shells
24 peeled prawns
fennel leaves
375 g (12 oz) smoked fish fillets, such as haddock, skinned and cut into pieces
3 egg whites
250 ml (8 fl oz/1 cup) double (thick) cream
salt
pinch of cayenne pepper
lime slices, lumpfish roe and sprigs of dill, to garnish

In a large saucepan of boiling salted water, cook pasta shells until tender. Drain.

Butter 6 individual ramekin dishes. Place 4 prawns and a piece of fennel in the bottom of each dish.

Preheat oven to 180C (350F/Gas 4). In a blender or food processor, process fish until smooth. Mix in egg whites and cream. Season with salt and cayenne pepper. Stir in pasta shells.

Divide mixture between ramekin dishes. Place dishes in a roasting tin. Pour in water to come halfway up dishes. Cook in the oven for about 15 minutes, or until firm. Turn out onto serving plates and garnish with lime slices, lumpfish roe and dill.

Serves 6 as a first course.

TUNA & MACARONI LAYER

185 g (6 oz/1¼ cups) wholewheat macaroni
90 g (3 oz/¾ cup) grated Cheddar cheese
220 g (7 oz) can tuna fish
½ quantity Béchamel Sauce
2 teaspoons lemon juice
2 hard-boiled eggs, chopped
3 teaspoons chopped fresh parsley
salt and pepper
lemon slices and sprigs of parsley, to garnish

In a large saucepan of boiling salted water, cook macaroni until tender. Drain and mix with 60 g (2 oz/½ cup) cheese.

Meanwhile, drain tuna fish. Flake into a saucepan with Béchamel sauce, lemon juice, chopped eggs and parsley and season with salt and pepper. Mix gently together. Cook over a low heat until warmed through.

Divide tuna mixture between 4 individual flameproof bowls or casserole dishes. Top with macaroni and cheese. Sprinkle remaining cheese over the top. Brown under a medium grill until golden and bubbling. Serve, garnished with lemon slices cut into triangles and sprigs of parsley.

Serves 4.

KIDNEY & PASTA TURBIGO

4 lamb's kidneys
60 g (2 oz/¼ cup) butter
8 cocktail sausages
125 g (4 oz) button mushrooms
24 button onions, peeled
1 teaspoon tomato purée (paste)
2 teaspoons plain flour
155 ml (5 fl oz/⅔ cup) beef stock
3 teaspoons dry sherry
1 bay leaf
salt and pepper
185 g (6 oz/3 cups) pasta spirals
sprigs of thyme, to garnish

Cut kidneys in half and remove core from each one.

In a saucepan, melt butter. Add kidneys and sausages. Cook, stirring occasionally, until brown. Remove from pan and set aside. Add mushrooms and onions to pan. Cook for 5-6 minutes, stirring occasionally.

Stir in tomato purée (paste) and flour. Cook for 1-2 minutes. Stir in stock and sherry. Bring to the boil. Return kidneys and sausages to pan with bay leaf. Season with salt and pepper. Cover pan and simmer for 20-25 minutes.

Meanwhile, in a large pan of boiling salted water, cook pasta until tender. Drain. Stir into kidney mixture. Serve, garnished with sprigs of thyme.

Serves 3-4.

COURGETTE PASTA BAKE

3 courgettes (zucchini), sliced
375 g (12 oz/4 cups) rigatoni
1 quantity Tomato Sauce
250 g (8 oz) Mozzarella cheese, thinly sliced
1 teaspoon olive oil
sprigs of basil, to garnish

In a saucepan of boiling water, cook sliced courgettes (zucchini) for a few minutes until cooked but still firm. Drain and set aside.

Preheat oven to 180C (350F/Gas 4). Butter an ovenproof dish. Meanwhile, in a large pan of boiling salted water, cook rigatoni until almost tender. Drain and rinse in cold water. Place a third of the rigatoni in the dish.

Spread a third of the tomato sauce over the rigatoni, followed by a third of the Mozzarella cheese. Repeat layers; spread courgettes (zucchini) over Mozzarella.

Cover with remaining rigatoni, tomato sauce and Mozzarella. Sprinkle with olive oil. Bake in the oven for 20 minutes until Mozzarella cheese has melted over the top. Serve, garnished with basil.

Serves 4-6.

PORK & BEANS

6 teaspoons vegetable oil	
375 g (12 oz) pork fillet, cut into thin slices	
1 onion, chopped	
1 clove garlic, crushed	
185 g (6 oz/1¼ cups) wholewheat pasta grills	
440 g (14 oz/1¾ cups) can cannellini beans	
9 teaspoons chopped fresh parsley	
9 teaspoons tomato purée (paste)	
1 litre (32 fl oz/4 cups) Chicken Stock	
salt and pepper	
chopped fresh parsley, to garnish	

In a saucepan, heat oil. Add pork, in batches, and fry until browned.

Remove pork from pan and set aside. Add onion and garlic to pan and cook until beginning to soften. Return pork to pan, stir in pasta, drained beans, parsley, tomato purée (paste) and stock and season with salt and pepper.

Bring to the boil. Cover pan and simmer, stirring occasionally, for about 20 minutes, or until pasta is tender and most of the liquid absorbed. Add more stock if liquid is absorbed before pasta is cooked. Transfer to a warmed serving dish and garnish with chopped parsley. Serve at once.

Serves 4.

DEVILLED CRAB

60 g (2 oz/1 cup) small pasta shells	
250 g (8 oz/1¾ cups) crabmeat	
1 teaspoon Dijon mustard	
2 teaspoons Worcestershire sauce	
juice of ½ a lemon	
125 ml (4 fl oz/½ cup) natural yogurt	
salt and cayenne pepper	
6 teaspoons fresh breadcrumbs	
30 g (1 oz/¼ cup) grated Parmesan cheese	
strips of lemon peel and whole fresh chives, to garnish	

In a large saucepan of boiling salted water, cook pasta shells until tender. Drain.

In a bowl, combine crabmeat, mustard, Worcestershire sauce, lemon juice, yogurt and pasta. Season with salt and cayenne pepper.

Grease 6 scallop shells and divide mixture between them. In a bowl, mix together breadcrumbs and Parmesan cheese.

Sprinkle crumbs over crab mixture. Cook under a medium grill for about 10 minutes, or until golden. Serve at once, garnished with strips of lemon peel and whole chives.

Serves 6 as a first course.

FRANKFURTER BAKE

6 teaspoons vegetable oil
1 onion, sliced
2 sticks celery, sliced
6 frankfurters, cut into 2.5 cm (1 in) lengths
2 tomatoes, skinned and chopped
185 g (6 oz/3 cups) pasta wheels
2 teaspoons cornflour
155 ml (5 fl oz/⅔ cup) thick sour cream
1 tablespoon tomato purée (paste)
salt and pepper
sprigs of parsley and thick sour cream, to serve, if desired

In a large frying pan, heat oil. Add onion, celery and frankfurters. Cook, stirring occasionally, until onion and celery are soft. Add tomatoes and cook for a further 5 minutes.

Preheat oven to 220C (425F/Gas 7). Meanwhile, in a large pan of boiling salted water, cook pasta.

In a bowl, blend cornflour and a little sour cream. Stir in remaining cream. Add to vegetables in frying pan with tomato purée (paste). Season with salt and pepper.

Drain pasta wheels and stir into vegetable mixture. Pour into an ovenproof dish and bake in the oven for 10 minutes. Serve at once, garnished with sprigs of parsley and sour cream, if desired.

Serves 4.

VERMICELLI TIMBALLO

125 g (4 oz) fine vermicelli
½ quantity Béchamel Sauce
30 g (1 oz/½ cup) fresh breadcrumbs
125 g (4 oz) Mozzarella cheese
125 g (4 oz) ham
sprigs of mint, to garnish
Tomato sauce

In a large saucepan of boiling salted water, cook vermicelli until just tender. Drain. In a bowl, combine vermicelli and Béchamel sauce. Set aside.

Preheat oven to 220C (425F/Gas 7). Butter six 155 ml (5 fl oz/⅔ cup) moulds or ovenproof teacups. Coat with half the breadcrumbs.

Cut Mozzarella cheese and ham into small dice. Half fill each mould with pasta mixture. Divide Mozzarella and ham between moulds.

Fill moulds with remaining pasta mixture. Sprinkle the tops with remaining breadcrumbs.

Bake in the oven for 15 minutes. Run a sharp knife around inside of the moulds. Turn out onto warmed serving plates. Garnish each plate with a sprig of mint and serve with tomato sauce.

Serves 6.

BAKED COD ITALIENNE

- 30 g (1 oz/6 teaspoons) butter
- 125 g (4 oz) mushrooms, sliced
- 1 quantity Tomato Sauce
- 4 white fish steaks, such as cod
- salt and pepper
- 125 g (4 oz/2 cups) pasta shells
- 8 black olives and sprigs of watercress, to garnish

Preheat oven to 190C (375F/Gas 5). In a saucepan, melt butter. Add mushrooms and cook gently until soft. Stir in tomato sauce.

Put fish in a shallow ovenproof dish. Season with salt and pepper. Pour over tomato and mushroom sauce. Cover dish and bake in the oven for about 25 minutes, or until fish flakes when tested with a fork.

Meanwhile, cook pasta shells until just tender. Five minutes before the end of the baking time, arrange pasta round fish, spooning some of the sauce over it. Garnish with black olives and sprigs of watercress and serve.

Serves 4.

BROCCOLI PASTA SOUFFLÉ

- 250 g (8 oz) broccoli
- 125 g (4 oz/2 cups) pasta shells
- 45 g (1½ oz/9 teaspoons) butter
- 45 g (1½ oz/⅓ cup) plain flour
- 315 ml (10 fl oz/1¼ cups) milk
- 90 g (3 oz/¾ cup) grated Cheddar cheese
- salt and pepper
- freshly grated nutmeg
- 3 eggs, separated, plus 1 extra egg white

Divide broccoli into small flowerets. Cook in boiling salted water until just tender but still crisp. Drain.

In a large saucepan of boiling salted water, cook pasta shells until tender.

Preheat oven to 200C (400F/Gas 6). Grease a 1 litre (32 fl oz/4 cup) soufflé dish. In a saucepan, melt butter and stir in flour. Cook for 2 minutes, stirring over gentle heat. Gradually add milk and cook, stirring, until sauce thickens. Simmer gently for 5 minutes, then stir in grated cheese. Season with salt, pepper and nutmeg. Leave for a few minutes to cool slightly.

In a large bowl, whisk egg whites until stiff but not dry. Stir egg yolks into cheese sauce, then add broccoli and pasta. Stir 1 tablespoon of egg white into mixture, then gently fold in the rest. Pour mixture into soufflé dish. Bake in the oven for about 30 minutes until the soufflé is well risen, golden brown and just set in the middle. Serve at once.

Serves 4.

Note: This mixture may be cooked in individual soufflé dishes and baked for 20 minutes.

BOLOGNESE SOUFFLÉ

185 g (6 oz/3 cups) wholewheat pasta spirals
1 quantity Bolognese Sauce
3 eggs, separated
30 g (1 oz/¼ cup) grated Parmesan cheese

Preheat oven to 190C (375F/Gas 5). Grease a 940 ml (30 fl oz/3¾ cup) soufflé dish. In a large saucepan of boiling salted water, cook pasta spirals until tender. Drain well. Stir into bolognese sauce.

Stir egg yolks into pasta mixture. In a bowl, beat egg whites until stiff but not dry. Stir 1 tablespoon of egg white into mixture, then gently fold in the rest.

Pour soufflé mixture into dish. Sprinkle with grated Parmesan cheese. Bake in the oven for 40 minutes, or until well risen and golden brown. Serve at once.

Serves 4.

Note: This mixture may be cooked in individual soufflé dishes and baked in the oven for 30 minutes.

PEPPER GRATIN

2 large red peppers (capsicums)
2 large yellow peppers (capsicums)
125 ml (4 fl oz/½ cup) olive oil
1 clove garlic, crushed
4 canned anchovies, drained and chopped
8 black olives, stoned and chopped
3 teaspoons capers
salt and pepper
250 g (8 oz) spaghetti
6 teaspoons fresh breadcrumbs
6 teaspoons Parmesan cheese, grated
strips of green pepper (capsicum) and black olives, to garnish

Cook peppers (capsicums) under a hot grill. Turn them at intervals until the skins are blistered and blackened.

Preheat the oven to 190C (375F/Gas 5). Grease an ovenproof dish. Scrape skins off peppers (capsicums). Cut peppers (capsicums) into strips. In a frying pan, heat half oil. Add strips of pepper (capsicum) and garlic. Cook for 2-3 minutes until peppers (capsicums) soften. Stir in anchovies, olives and capers and season with salt and pepper.

Meanwhile, in a large saucepan of boiling salted water cook spaghetti until tender. Drain, return to pan; toss with half remaining olive oil. Combine breadcrumbs and Parmesan and sprinkle half over base of dish. Cover with half the pepper (capsicum) mixture, then with spaghetti. Cover with remaining pepper (capsicum) mixture. Sprinkle with remaining crumbs and cheese. Pour over remaining oil. Bake in the oven for 20 minutes, or until brown and crisp. Serve at once, garnished with strips of green pepper (capsicum) and black olives.

Serves 4.

TURKEY TETRAZZINI

250 g (8 oz) red, green and white tagliatelle
60 g (2 oz/¼ cup) butter
4 rashers streaky bacon, rinds removed, chopped
1 onion, finely chopped
125 g (4 oz) mushrooms, sliced
45 g (1½ oz/⅓ cup) plain flour
440 ml (14 fl oz/1¾ cups) Chicken Stock
155 ml (5 fl oz/⅔ cup) double (thick) cream
6 teaspoons dry sherry
375 g (12 oz) cooked turkey, cubed
salt and pepper
freshly grated nutmeg
30 g (1 oz/¼ cup) grated Parmesan cheese
sprig of parsley, to garnish

Preheat oven to 180C (350F/Gas 4). In a large saucepan of boiling salted water, cook tagliatelle until tender. Drain.

In a saucepan, melt butter. Add bacon and onion and cook until onion is soft. Add the sliced mushrooms and cook until mushrooms are just soft.

Stir in flour. Gradually stir in stock, bring to boil and simmer, stirring, until sauce is thickened and smooth. Remove pan from the heat. Stir in cream, sherry, turkey and tagliatelle. Season with salt, pepper and nutmeg. Pour into an ovenproof dish. Sprinkle with Parmesan cheese. Bake in the oven for 30 minutes, or until the top is golden brown. Serve at once, garnished with a sprig of parsley.

Serves 4.

SWEET & SOUR PORK

1 kg (2 lb) boned belly of pork, trimmed of excess fat
6 teaspoons vegetable oil
1 onion, sliced
1 teaspoon ground ginger
3 teaspoons plain flour
250 g (8 oz) can pineapple pieces in natural juice
315 ml (10 fl oz/1¼ cups) Chicken Stock
315 ml (10 fl oz/1¼ cups) dry cider
6 teaspoons soy sauce
2 teaspoons Worcestershire sauce
6 teaspoons soft brown sugar
6 teaspoons wine vinegar
salt and pepper
60 g (2 oz/1 cup) small pasta shells
slices of green pepper (capsicum) and spring onion tassels, to garnish

Preheat oven to 150C (300F/Gas 2). Cut pork into 2.5 cm (1 in) cubes. Heat oil in a flameproof casserole.

Add the pork and cook until well browned. Remove from casserole and set aside. Add onion to casserole. Cook until soft. Stir in ginger and flour. Cook mixture for 1 minute.

Drain juice from pineapple. Set pineapple aside. Add juice to casserole with stock, cider, soy sauce, Worcestershire sauce, sugar and vinegar. Season with salt and pepper. Stir well. Return meat to casserole. Cover and cook in the oven for 1 hour. Add pineapple and pasta. Cover and cook for 45 minutes, or until pasta is tender. Serve at once, garnished with slices of green pepper (capsicum) and spring onion tassels.

Serves 4-6.

FISH & PASTA PIE

375 g (12 oz) smoked haddock	
375 g (12 oz) fresh haddock	
440 ml (14 fl oz/1¾ cups) milk	
185 g (6 oz/1¼ cups) macaroni	
30 g (1 oz/6 teaspoons) butter	
30 g (1 oz/¼ cup) plain flour	
1 teaspoon lemon juice	
3 hard-boiled eggs, sliced	
3 teaspoons chopped fresh parsley	
salt and pepper	
250 ml (8 fl oz/1 cup) Greek strained yogurt	
2 eggs, beaten	
90 g (3 oz/¾ cup) grated Cheddar cheese	
lemon slices and sprigs of parsley, to garnish	

Put fresh and smoked haddock in a saucepan with milk and 315 ml (10 fl oz/1¼ cups) water. Poach fish for 5-10 minutes until flesh flakes when tested with a fork.

In a large saucepan of boiling salted water, cook macaroni until tender.

Preheat oven to 190C (375F/Gas 5). In a heavy saucepan, melt butter. Stir in flour and cook for 2 minutes, stirring over gentle heat. Remove from heat and stir in 315 ml (10 fl oz/1¼ cups) of cooking liquid. Return to heat and stir until thick and smooth. Add lemon juice, hard-boiled eggs, and parsley. Season with salt and pepper. Pour mixture into an ovenproof dish.

In a bowl, mix together yogurt and beaten eggs. Stir in macaroni and 60 g (2 oz/½ cup) cheese. Pour over fish mixture. Sprinkle with remaining cheese. Bake in the oven for 25-30 minutes until golden brown. Serve, garnished with lemon slices and sprigs of parsley.

Serves 4-6.

ORIENTAL LAMB CASSEROLE

750 g (1½ lb) boned shoulder of lamb
1 green pepper (capsicum), seeded
1 red pepper (capsicum), seeded
3 teaspoons vegetable oil
1 onion, cut into wedges
1 carrot, cut into matchsticks
375 g (12 oz) white cabbage, shredded
6 teaspoons soy sauce
3 teaspoons Worcestershire sauce
6 teaspoons white wine vinegar
3 teaspoons clear honey
500 ml (16 fl oz/2 cups) light stock
3 teaspoons chopped fresh parsley
salt and pepper
60 g (2 oz) round egg noodles
crispy noodles and chopped fresh parsley, to garnish

Cut lamb into 2.5 cm (1 in) cubes. Cut peppers (capsicums) into strips. Heat oil in a flameproof casserole, add lamb and cook until brown.

Add onion, carrot, peppers (capsicums) and cabbage to casserole. Stir well, then cook gently for 5 minutes. In a bowl, mix together soy sauce, Worcestershire sauce, vinegar, honey and stock. Stir into casserole. Stir in parsley and season.

Cover casserole and cook for about 50 minutes, stirring occasionally. Add noodles and cook for a further 10 minutes. Serve, garnished with crispy noodles and parsley.

Serves 4.

STUFFED PEPPERS

- 60 g (2 oz/1 cup) pasta spirals
- ½ quantity Tomato Sauce
- 2 teaspoons capers
- 6 black olives, stoned and chopped
- 2 red peppers (capsicums)
- 2 yellow peppers (capsicums)
- 2 teaspoons olive oil
- sprig of basil, to garnish

Preheat oven to 190C (375F/Gas 5). Grease an ovenproof dish. In a large saucepan of boiling salted water, cook pasta spirals until tender. Drain.

In a bowl, mix together pasta, tomato sauce, capers and olives.

Slice off the stalk end of peppers (capsicums). Remove core and seeds. Fill peppers (capsicums) with pasta and tomato mixture. Replace tops of peppers (capsicums).

Stand peppers (capsicums) in the ovenproof dish. Pour a little olive oil over each one. Cook in oven for about 30 minutes, or until peppers (capsicums) are tender. Serve, garnished with a sprig of basil.

Serves 4.

BEEF & MACARONI STRUDEL

- 90 g (3 oz/⅓ cup) butter
- 30 g (1 oz/¼ cup) plain flour
- 185 ml (6 fl oz/¾ cup) milk
- salt and pepper
- 125 g (4 oz/1 cup) macaroni
- 6 teaspoons vegetable oil
- 1 onion, finely chopped
- 250 g (8 oz) ground beef
- 3 teaspoons tomato purée (paste)
- ½ teaspoon ground cinnamon
- 3 teaspoons chopped fresh parsley
- 4 sheets filo pastry
- tomato slices, onion rings and sprigs of parsley, to garnish

In a saucepan, make a Béchamel sauce, see page 28, with 30 g (1 oz/6 teaspoons) butter, the flour and milk. Season with salt and pepper.

In a large saucepan of boiling salted water, cook macaroni. Preheat oven to 190C (375F/Gas 5). Meanwhile, in a frying pan, heat oil. Add onion and cook until soft. Add ground beef and stir until well browned. Stir in tomato purée (paste), cinnamon and parsley. Season. Drain macaroni, then stir into beef mixture with sauce.

In a small saucepan, melt remaining butter. Brush a sheet of filo pastry with butter. Lay another sheet of pastry on top. Brush with more butter. Repeat with remaining pastry. Place macaroni mixture in a line along one long edge of pastry, leaving a space at each end. Tuck ends over, then roll up firmly.

Place on a baking sheet. Brush roll with butter. Bake in the oven for 45 minutes, or until brown and crisp, brushing with butter occasionally. Garnish and serve.

Serves 4.

Variation: Make individual strudels and bake for 20–25 minutes.

MONGOLIAN HOT POT

- 60 g (2 oz) transparent noodles
- 500 g (1 lb) chicken breasts (fillets), skinned
- 500 g (1 lb) rump steak
- 250 g (8 oz/1 cup) can bamboo shoots, drained
- 125 g (4 oz) Chinese leaves, shredded
- 100 g (4 oz) button mushrooms
- 1.7 litres (60 fl oz/7½ cups) Chicken Stock
- 2.5 cm (1 in) piece fresh root ginger, peeled and grated
- 1 clove garlic, crushed
- 4 spring onions, chopped
- red chilli flowers and slices, to garnish

SAUCE:

- 6 teaspoons peanut butter
- 6 teaspoons soy sauce
- 6 teaspoons dry sherry
- pinch of chilli powder

In a bowl of warm water, soak noodles for 5 minutes. Drain.

Cut chicken, steak and bamboo shoots into very thin strips. Arrange on a flat dish with Chinese leaves and mushrooms.

To make sauce, mix peanut butter with 3 teaspoons hot water in a bowl. Stir in soy sauce, sherry and chilli powder. Divide sauce between 4 individual bowls. Garnish with chilli.

In a saucepan or fondue pot, bring chicken stock to the boil. Add ginger, garlic and spring onions. Put pot on a burner at the table. Dip meat and vegetables into stock to cook. Eat with sauce. Add noodles to stock. Allow to heat through. Serve stock in soup bowls.

Serves 4.

SPICY NOODLES

- 6 teaspoons vegetable oil
- 1 clove garlic, crushed
- 1 cm (½ in) piece fresh root ginger, peeled and grated
- 250 g (8 oz) spinach, roughly chopped
- 250 g (8 oz) white cabbage, shredded
- 315 ml (10 fl oz/1¼ cups) Chicken Stock
- 3 teaspoons soy sauce
- 1 teaspoon chilli sauce
- 125 g (4 oz) fine egg noodles

In a wok or large frying pan, heat oil. Add garlic and ginger. Cook, stirring, for 1 minute.

Add spinach and cabbage. Cook, stirring, until they are bright green and almost tender. Stir in stock, soy sauce and chilli sauce.

Stir in noodles and simmer for a few minutes until tender. Serve as an accompaniment.

Serves 4.

CHICKEN SUKIYAKI

125 g (4 oz) rice vermicelli
6 teaspoons vegetable oil
1 onion, finely chopped
1 leek, finely sliced
500 g (1 lb) skinned chicken breasts (fillets), cut into strips
125 g (4 oz) mushrooms, sliced
250 g (8 oz) tofu, cubed
250 ml (8 fl oz/1 cup) Chicken Stock
60 ml (2 fl oz/¼ cup) soy sauce
3 teaspoons sugar
sliced lotus root and sprigs of coriander, to garnish

Put vermicelli into a bowl. Pour over boiling water to cover. Leave to soak for 10 minutes. Drain thoroughly.

In a large heavy frying pan, heat oil. Add onion and leek and cook for a few minutes until beginning to soften. Add chicken and cook, stirring, until lightly browned. Stir in mushrooms and tofu.

In a bowl, mix together stock, soy sauce and sugar. Pour into pan and simmer gently for 10-15 minutes until chicken and vegetables are cooked. Stir in drained vermicelli and heat through. Serve, garnished with lotus root and coriander.

Serves 4.

Note: This recipe is an adaptation of traditional sukiyaki which refers to the method of cooking at the table in a large heavy pan. Diners help themselves to the cooked meat and vegetables, dipping them in beaten egg before eating them.

SPICY SESAME NOODLES

6 teaspoons sesame seeds
3 teaspoons sesame oil
4 teaspoons peanut butter
2 tablespoons soy sauce
2 teaspoons chilli sauce
½ teaspoon sugar
250 g (8 oz) rice vermicelli
carrot flowers and toasted sesame seeds, to garnish

In a dry frying pan, cook sesame seeds over a medium heat until golden brown. Crush slightly.

In a bowl, or food processor, mix together sesame seeds, sesame oil, peanut butter, soy sauce, chilli sauce, sugar and 60 ml (2 fl oz/¼ cup) water. Set aside.

Put rice vermicelli into a bowl. Pour over enough boiling water to cover. Leave to soak for 10 minutes, then drain thoroughly. Put drained vermicelli and sesame sauce into a saucepan. Mix together to coat vermicelli in sauce. Cook over a low heat until mixture is thoroughly heated through. Serve, garnished with carrot flowers and sesame seeds.

Serves 4.

SINGAPORE NOODLES

- 6 teaspoons vegetable oil
- 125 g (4 oz) mushrooms, sliced
- 1 onion, finely chopped
- 1 clove garlic, crushed
- 125 g (4 oz) ham, cut into shreds
- 2.5 cm (1 in) piece fresh root ginger, peeled and grated
- 50 g (2 oz / ½ cup) frozen peas
- 250 g (8 oz) rice vermicelli
- 125 g (4 oz) cooked chicken
- 1 teaspoon curry powder
- salt
- 125 g (4 oz) peeled prawns
- 75 ml (2½ fl oz/⅓ cup) Chicken Stock
- 4 teaspoons soy sauce
- 60 ml (2 fl oz/¼ cup) dry sherry
- spring onion tassels, to garnish

In a large frying pan, heat vegetable oil. Add mushrooms, onion, garlic, ham and ginger. Stir well. Cook over a low heat for 10 minutes. Add peas and cook for 5 minutes.

Put rice vermicelli in a bowl. Pour boiling water over, to cover. Leave to soak for 10 minutes. Drain thoroughly. Meanwhile, cut the chicken into matchstick pieces. Stir curry powder and salt into mushroom and ham mixture.

Add chicken, prawns, stock, soy sauce and sherry; stir thoroughly. Add noodles and heat gently. Garnish with spring onion tassels.

Serves 4.

NOODLES WITH EGGS

- 375 g (12 oz) buckwheat noodles
- 2 tablespoons vegetable oil
- 1 onion, chopped
- 185 g (6 oz) Chinese leaves, shredded
- 4 eggs, beaten
- 3 teaspoons soy sauce
- salt and pepper
- bay leaf and lemon peel rose, to garnish

In a large saucepan of boiling salted water, cook buckwheat noodles in the same way as spaghetti, until just tender.

Meanwhile, in a heavy saucepan, heat oil. Add onion and cook until soft. Add Chinese leaves and cook until beginning to soften, then stir in beaten eggs. Cook, stirring, for about 1 minute until eggs are beginning to set.

Drain noodles and stir into egg mixture. Add soy sauce and season with salt and pepper. Serve at once, garnished with a bay leaf and lemon peel rose.

Serves 4.

VERMICELLI & CHICK PEAS

- 125 g (4 oz/$\frac{2}{3}$ cup) chick peas, soaked overnight
- 60 g (2 oz/$\frac{1}{4}$ cup) butter
- 1 onion, finely chopped
- 185 g (6 oz) vermicelli
- 250 g (8 oz/$1\frac{3}{4}$ cups) long grain rice
- salt
- 75 ml ($2\frac{1}{2}$ fl oz/$\frac{1}{3}$ cup) thick sour cream
- sprig of parsley, to garnish

Drain chick peas and rinse in cold water. Put chick peas and 750 ml (24 fl oz/3 cups) water into a saucepan. Bring to boil, then cover pan and simmer for 30 minutes, or until chick peas are tender.

In a large saucepan, melt butter. Add onion and cook gently until tender. Break vermicelli into 2.5 cm (1 in) pieces and add to pan. Stir until well coated with butter. Add rice and cook, stirring, until grains are transparent. Add 625 ml (20 fl oz/$2\frac{1}{2}$ cups) water and salt to taste. Bring to boil, then cover pan tightly and simmer for about 25 minutes, or until water is absorbed and rice is tender. Add more water if it dries up before rice is cooked.

Stir chick peas into vermicelli and rice. Cook over a low heat until heated through. Pour sour cream over the top and serve, garnished with a sprig of parsley.

Serves 6.

GREEK RAVIOLI

- 1 egg
- 250 g (8 oz/2 cups) strong white flour
- 30 g (1 oz/6 teaspoons) butter

FILLING:

- 3 egg yolks
- 155 g (5 oz/$1\frac{1}{3}$ cups) grated Parmesan cheese
- 375 g (12 oz/3 cups) grated Greek Halumi cheese
- salt, pepper and freshly grated nutmeg
- black olives and oregano leaves, to garnish

Make a pasta dough with egg, flour and 75 ml ($2\frac{1}{2}$ fl oz/$\frac{1}{3}$ cup) water, see page 9. Wrap in a damp cloth.

In a blender or food processor, process egg yolks, 125 g (4 oz/1 cup) Parmesan cheese, the Halumi cheese, and salt, pepper and nutmeg to form a smooth paste. Roll out and fill pasta dough as for ravioli, see page 12.

Preheat oven to 190C (375F/Gas 5). Grease an ovenproof dish. In a large saucepan of boiling salted water, cook ravioli for 10-15 minutes, then drain. Arrange in the dish. Dot with butter and sprinkle with remaining Parmesan cheese. Bake in oven for 10-15 minutes until brown. Serve, garnished with black olives and oregano leaves.

Serves 4.

Variation: This recipe can be made with any of the pasta dough variations, see page 9, and made into other shapes, if preferred.

SPAGHETTI LAYER

- 2 aubergines (eggplants), sliced
- salt
- 500 g (1 lb) spaghetti
- olive oil
- 1 quantity Tomato Sauce
- 3 hard-boiled eggs, thinly sliced
- 90 g (3 oz/$^3/_4$ cup) grated Parmesan cheese
- chopped hard-boiled egg, to garnish

Put the sliced aubergines (eggplants) into a colander. Sprinkle with salt and leave to drain for at least 30 minutes.

In a large saucepan of boiling salted water, cook spaghetti until tender. Drain.

Preheat oven to 190C (375F/Gas 5). Grease an ovenproof dish. Remove aubergine (eggplant) slices from colander and pat dry. In a frying pan, heat 2 tablespoons olive oil. Fry aubergine (eggplant) slices in batches until very tender, adding more oil as necessary. Drain on absorbent kitchen paper.

In a bowl, mix together spaghetti and tomato sauce. Spread one-third of spaghetti mixture in the ovenproof dish. Cover with half the aubergine (eggplant) slices and half the hard-boiled egg slices. Sprinkle with one-third of the Parmesan cheese. Repeat layers then finish with a layer of spaghetti. Sprinkle with remaining Parmesan. Bake in the oven for 30 minutes until golden. Serve, garnished with chopped hard-boiled egg.

Serves 6.

JAPANESE NOODLES

- 6 teaspoons vegetable oil
- 1 onion, chopped
- 1 clove garlic, crushed
- 250 g (8 oz) chicken breasts (fillets), cut into small dice
- 1 carrot, cut into matchsticks
- 1 potato, cut into 1 cm ($^1/_2$ in) dice
- $^1/_2$ red pepper (capsicum), diced
- 1$^1/_2$ teaspoons curry powder
- 2.5 cm (1 in) piece fresh root ginger, peeled and grated
- salt
- 185 g (6 oz) noodles
- 2 spring onions, finely chopped, and spring onion tassels, to garnish

In a large saucepan, heat oil. Add onion and garlic and cook gently until tender. Add chicken, carrot, potato, and pepper (capsicum). Cook, stirring, until chicken begins to brown.

Stir in curry powder and ginger. Add 155 ml (5 fl oz/$^2/_3$ cup) water. Cover pan and cook, stirring occasionally, until vegetables are tender and sauce has thickened. Season with salt.

Meanwhile, in a large saucepan of boiling salted water, cook noodles until tender. Drain thoroughly.

Stir noodles into chicken mixture. Cook for a few minutes over a gentle heat until heated through. Serve in individual bowls, garnished with chopped spring onion and spring onion tassels.

Serves 4.

MOROCCAN MACARONI PIE

4 teaspoons vegetable oil
1 onion, finely chopped
1 clove garlic, crushed
375 g (12 oz) shoulder of lamb
440 g (14 oz) can chopped tomatoes
6 teaspoons tomato purée (paste)
½ teaspoon ground cinnamon
½ teaspoon ground cumin
salt and pepper
375 g (12 oz/2½ cups) macaroni
8 sheets filo pastry
60 g (2 oz/¼ cup) butter, melted
sprig of parsley, to garnish

In a saucepan, heat oil. Add onion and garlic. Cook gently until soft.

Cut lamb into small cubes. Add to onion and fry, stirring, until brown. Stir in tomatoes, tomato purée (paste), cinnamon and cumin. Season with salt and pepper. Cover and simmer for 1½ hours, or until lamb is tender and sauce is thick.

Meanwhile, in a large saucepan of boiling salted water, cook macaroni until tender. Drain. Stir into meat. Preheat oven to 220C (425F/Gas 7). Grease an ovenproof dish.

Line the dish with a sheet of filo pastry, leaving the edges overhanging the dish. Brush pastry with melted butter. Repeat with 3 more sheets of pastry.

Fill dish with macaroni mixture. Top with 4 more sheets of pastry, brushing each one with melted butter. Tuck edges of pastry down sides of dish. Brush top with melted butter. Bake in the oven for 15 minutes. Lower oven temperature to 160C (325F/Gas 3). Bake for 30 minutes longer, until pastry is cooked and the top is crisp. Serve, garnished with a sprig of parsley.

Serves 4-6.

CRABMEAT & NOODLES

250 g (8 oz) egg noodles
2 tablespoons vegetable oil
250 g (8 oz) fresh crabmeat or frozen crabmeat, thawed
250 g (8 oz) Chinese leaves, roughly shredded
4 teaspoons chilli bean sauce
2 teaspoons soy sauce
250 ml (8 fl oz/1 cup) light stock
2 spring onions, finely chopped

In a large saucepan of boiling, salted water, cook noodles until just tender. Drain thoroughly. Put onto a hot serving dish and keep warm.

In a wok or large frying pan, heat oil. Stir-fry crabmeat and Chinese leaves for 2 minutes. Add chilli bean sauce, soy sauce and stock. Cook for 2-3 minutes.

Pour sauce over noodles. Garnish with spring onions. Serve at once.

Serves 4.

CHOW MEIN

- 250 g (8 oz) Chinese egg noodles
- 185 g (6 oz) pork fillet
- 1 teaspoon cornflour
- 4 teaspoons light soy sauce
- 2 teaspoons dry sherry
- 6 teaspoons vegetable oil for frying
- 60 g (2 oz) mange-tout (snow peas), trimmed
- $\frac{1}{2}$ a cucumber, cut into matchsticks
- 1 spring onion, finely chopped
- 1 teaspoon sesame oil
- cucumber slices, to garnish

Cook noodles according to directions on packet. Drain, rinse with cold water, then leave to drain.

Cut pork fillet into matchstick shreds. In a bowl, mix together pork, cornflour, 2 teaspoons soy sauce and sherry. Leave to marinate for 10 minutes.

In a wok or frying pan, heat half vegetable oil. Add noodles and stir-fry for 2-3 minutes. Remove to a warmed serving dish and keep warm. Heat remaining vegetable oil in wok or pan.

Over a high heat, stir-fry pork, mange-tout (snow peas) and cucumber for 4-5 minutes. Stir in remaining soy sauce. Pour over noodles. Sprinkle chopped spring onions and sesame oil over top. Serve at once, garnished with cucumber slices.

Serves 4.

FRIED WONTON

- 250 g (8 oz/2 cups) strong white bread flour
- 1 egg
- vegetable oil for deep frying
- chilli flower, to garnish

FILLING:

- 125 g (4 oz) frozen chopped spinach
- 250 g (8 oz) minced pork
- 3 teaspoons soy sauce
- 3 teaspoons dry sherry
- 2 spring onions, finely chopped
- 2.5 cm (1 in) piece fresh root ginger, peeled and grated
- 1 egg, beaten
- $\frac{1}{2}$ teaspoon cornflour

Mix together flour, egg and 75 ml ($2\frac{1}{2}$ fl oz/$\frac{1}{3}$ cup) water to make a pasta dough, see page 9. Wrap in a damp cloth.

Meanwhile, make filling. Cook frozen spinach, drain and put into a bowl. Add pork, soy sauce, sherry, spring onions, ginger, egg and cornflour. Mix together thoroughly.

To make wonton skins, roll out dough, see page 10. Cut into 7.5 cm (3 in) squares. Put a teaspoon of filling in the middle of each square. Pinch top edges firmly together to seal. In a deep fat fryer, heat oil to 190C (375F) until cube of day-old bread turns golden in 40 seconds.

Fry the wonton in several batches until brown and crisp. Drain on absorbent kitchen paper. Serve at once, garnished with a chilli flower, with a hot chilli sauce.

Makes about 24.

Note: You can buy ready-made fresh or frozen wonton skins from Chinese grocers.

VEGETABLE CASSEROLE

- 2 tablespoons vegetable oil
- 1 onion, finely sliced
- 2 teaspoons plain flour
- 1 tablespoon paprika
- 440 g (14 oz) can tomatoes
- 250 g (8 oz) cauliflower flowerets
- 2 carrots, roughly chopped
- ½ green pepper (capsicum), seeded and roughly chopped
- 2 courgettes (zucchini), roughly chopped
- 125 g (4 oz/2 cups) wholewheat pasta shells
- salt and pepper
- 155 ml (5 fl oz/⅔ cup) Greek strained yogurt
- sprig of parsley, to garnish

In a saucepan, heat oil. Add onion and cook until soft.

Stir in flour and paprika. Cook, stirring, for 1 minute. Add tomatoes and 315 ml (10 fl oz/1¼ cups) water. Bring to the boil, then stir in cauliflower, carrots, green pepper (capsicum), courgettes (zucchini) and pasta. Season with salt and pepper. Cover pan and simmer for 40 minutes, or until pasta is tender.

Gently stir yogurt into vegetable mixture and serve, garnished with a sprig of parsley.

Serves 4.

MACARONI BAKE

- 125 g (4 oz) leeks, thinly sliced
- 125 g (4 oz/¾ cup) wholewheat macaroni
- 2 sticks celery
- 1 red pepper (capsicum)
- 155 ml (5 fl oz/⅔ cup) natural yogurt
- 125 g (4 oz/) low fat soft cheese
- 2 teaspoons naturally fermented shoyu (soy sauce)
- salt and pepper
- 60 g (2 oz/½ cup) grated Cheddar cheese

Preheat oven to 180C (350F/Gas 4). Put leeks into a saucepan of boiling water. Bring back to the boil. Drain.

In a large saucepan of boiling salted water, cook macaroni until tender. Drain.

Finely chop celery and red pepper (capsicum). In a bowl, mix together leeks, celery, red pepper (capsicum) and macaroni.

In a bowl, mix together yogurt, low fat soft cheese and shoyu. Season with salt and pepper. Pour over macaroni mixture. Mix together thoroughly. Put into an ovenproof dish and sprinkle grated cheese over top. Bake in the oven for 30 minutes until golden and bubbling.

Serves 4.

VEGETARIAN BOLOGNESE

185 g (6 oz/1 cup) brown lentils	
125 g (4 oz/⅔ cup) split peas	
2 tablespoons vegetable oil	
1 onion, finely chopped	
1 clove garlic, crushed	
1 carrot, finely chopped	
1 stick celery, finely chopped	
440 g (14 oz) can tomatoes	
1 teaspoon dried oregano	
salt and pepper	
Parmesan cheese, to serve	
sprig of parsley, to garnish	

In a saucepan, bring 625 ml (20 fl oz/2½ cups) water to the boil. Stir in lentils and split peas. Simmer, covered, for about 40 minutes, or until all liquid has been absorbed and lentils and peas are soft.

In a saucepan, heat oil. Add onion, garlic, carrot and celery. Cook over a low heat, stirring occasionally, until soft. Stir in chopped tomatoes and oregano. Season with salt and pepper. Cover pan and simmer gently for 5 minutes.

Add lentils and split peas to pan. Cook, stirring, until well combined and heated through. Serve with wholewheat spaghetti sprinkled with Parmesan cheese and garnished with parsley.

Serves 4-6.

PASTA & VEGETABLE LOAF

125 g (4 oz/⅔ cup) brown lentils	
125 g (4 oz/⅔ cup) split peas	
125 g (4 oz/2 cups) small wholewheat pasta shapes	
125 g (4 oz/½ cup) butter	
1 onion, chopped	
1 clove garlic, crushed	
1 large carrot, scrubbed and chopped	
1 stick celery, chopped	
1 egg, beaten	
½ teaspoon ground cumin	
2 tablespoons chopped fresh parsley	
salt and pepper	
sprig of mint, to garnish	

In a saucepan, bring 625 ml (20 fl oz/2½ cups) water to the boil. Stir in lentils and split peas. Simmer, covered, for about 40 minutes, or until all liquid has been absorbed and lentils and peas are soft.

Meanwhile, preheat oven to 190C (375F/Gas 5). Grease a 500 g (1 lb) loaf tin. In a large saucepan of boiling salted water, cook pasta shapes until tender.

In a saucepan, heat butter. Add onion, garlic, carrot and celery. Cook, stirring occasionally, until soft. Add lentils, split peas, pasta, beaten egg, cumin and parsley. Season with salt and pepper.

Mix together thoroughly. Spoon mixture into the loaf tin. Cover with foil. Bake in the oven for 40 minutes. Leave in tin for 5 minutes, then run a knife round edge of loaf and turn out onto a serving dish. Serve sliced, garnished with mint.

Serves 4.

Note: This loaf may be served hot with tomato sauce or cold with salad.

VEGETARIAN LASAGNE

- 185 g (6 oz/1 cup) aduki beans, soaked overnight
- 6-8 sheets wholewheat lasagne
- 2 tablespoons vegetable oil
- 1 onion, finely chopped
- 1 clove garlic, crushed
- 250 g (8 oz) white cabbage, shredded
- 125 g (4 oz) mushrooms, sliced
- 1 leek, roughly chopped
- ½ green pepper (capsicum), chopped
- 440 g (14 oz) can tomatoes
- 1 teaspoon dried oregano
- salt and pepper
- 1 quantity Béchamel Sauce made with wholewheat flour
- 60 g (2 oz/½ cup) grated Cheddar cheese
- sprigs of watercress, to garnish

Drain aduki beans. Put into a saucepan with 1 litre (32 fl oz/4 cups) water. Bring to boil, cover pan and cook for 40 minutes.

In a large saucepan of boiling salted water, cook lasagne until tender. Drain and pat dry. In a saucepan, heat oil. Add onion and garlic and cook until soft. Stir in cabbage, mushrooms, leek, and pepper (capsicum) and cook for 5 minutes, stirring occasionally. Drain aduki beans, reserving cooking water, and add to vegetables.

Stir in tomatoes and 185 ml (6 fl oz/1 cup) cooking water from beans. Add oregano and season with salt and pepper. Cover pan and simmer gently for 30 minutes, stirring occasionally.

Preheat oven to 180C (350F/Gas 4). In an ovenproof baking dish, make layers of lasagne, vegetables and sauce, ending with a layer of sauce. Sprinkle grated cheese over top. Bake in the oven for 30 minutes until golden. Serve, garnished with watercress, with salad.

Serves 4-6.

PASTA PAN FRY

- 250 g (8 oz/4 cups) pasta bows
- 2 tablespoons vegetable oil
- 1 onion, chopped
- 1 green pepper (capsicum), seeded and chopped
- 125 g (4 oz) mushrooms, sliced
- 250 g (8 oz) chicken livers, chopped
- 250 g (8 oz) tomatoes, peeled and chopped
- 2 fresh sage leaves, chopped
- salt and pepper
- sage leaves, to garnish

In a large saucepan of boiling salted water, cook pasta bows until tender. Drain.

In a large frying pan, heat the oil. Add onion and cook for a few minutes until soft.

Add green pepper (capsicum) and cook, stirring, for 3 minutes. Add mushrooms and cook, stirring, for a further 2 minutes. Add chicken livers and stir-fry until livers are no longer pink.

Stir tomatoes and sage into chicken liver mixture and season with salt and pepper. Cook, stirring, until the juice begins to run from tomatoes. Add pasta bows and heat. Serve, garnished with sage leaves.

Serves 3-4.

GOLDEN FRITTERS

60g (2 oz/$\frac{1}{2}$ cup) macaroni
2 eggs
125 g (4 oz/1 cup) grated Cheddar cheese
60 g (2 oz/$\frac{2}{3}$ cup) canned sweetcorn, drained
salt and pepper
vegetable oil for frying
sprigs of parsley, to garnish

In a large saucepan of boiling salted water, cook macaroni until tender. Drain and rinse thoroughly with cold water.

In a bowl, beat eggs, add macaroni, cheese and sweetcorn. Season to taste with salt and pepper and stir thoroughly.

In a frying pan, heat oil. Drop in tablespoons of macaroni mixture. Fry until each fritter is crisp and golden on the underside and the upper side is set. Turn and fry until the other side is crisp and golden. Drain on absorbent kitchen paper and serve garnished with parsley.

Serves 4.

DEEP-FRIED RAVIOLI

250 g (8 oz) frozen chopped spinach, cooked and drained
250 g (8 oz) cooked chicken
2 egg yolks
60 g (2 oz/$\frac{1}{2}$ cup) grated Parmesan cheese
salt and pepper
freshly grated nutmeg
3-egg quantity Pasta Dough
vegetable oil for deep frying
lime and lemon slices and sprigs of parsley, to garnish

Squeeze as much water as possible from spinach. In a blender or food processor, process chicken, spinach, egg yolks, Parmesan cheese, salt, pepper and nutmeg until quite smooth.

Roll out pasta dough. Using chicken mixture as a filling, make ravioli.

In a deep fat fryer, heat oil to 190C (375F) or until a cube of day-old bread browns in 40 seconds. Fry ravioli, in batches, until crisp and golden brown. Drain on absorbent kitchen paper and keep hot until all the ravioli are cooked. Serve at once, garnished with lime and lemon slices and sprigs of parsley.

Serves 4.

PIZZA-STYLE SPAGHETTINI

250 g (8 oz) spaghettini
125 g (4 oz/1 cup) grated Cheddar cheese
2 eggs, beaten
125 g (4 oz) salami, diced
½ teaspoon dried oregano
salt and pepper
vegetable oil for frying
2 tomatoes, sliced
6 black olives
sprigs of oregano, to garnish

In a large saucepan of boiling salted water, cook spaghettini until tender. Drain and rinse with cold water.

In a bowl, using hands, mix spaghettini, cheese, eggs, salami, and oregano thoroughly together. Season with salt and pepper.

In a frying pan, heat oil. Tip spaghettini mixture into pan and pat out evenly. Cook for about 5 minutes until the underside is brown and crisp, and the top is set.

Turn over onto a plate, then slide back into pan. Cook second side until brown and crisp. Turn onto a large serving plate and arrange tomato slices and olives on top. Garnish with sprigs of oregano.

Serves 4-6.

CRISPY CANNELLONI

8 cannelloni tubes
2 tablespoons vegetable oil
1 leek, finely chopped
250 g (8 oz) low fat soft cheese
125 g (4 oz) mortadella, chopped
1 teaspoon tomato purée (paste)
2 eggs
1 tablespoon chopped fresh parsley
salt and pepper
5 tablespoons fresh breadcrumbs
5 tablespoons grated Parmesan cheese
vegetable oil for deep frying
lemon slices and sprigs of parsley, to garnish

In a large saucepan of salted water, cook cannelloni for 4-5 minutes until almost soft. Drain cannelloni, rinse with cold water and spread out on a tea towel.

In a frying pan, heat oil. Fry chopped leek until soft. In a bowl, mix together leek, soft cheese, mortadella, tomato purée (paste), 1 egg and parsley. Season with salt and pepper.

Using a small teaspoon, push filling into cannelloni. Mix together breadcrumbs and Parmesan cheese. Spread out on a large plate. Beat remaining egg in a shallow dish. Roll cannelloni in beaten egg and coat with breadcrumb mixture.

In a deep fat fryer, heat oil to 190C (375F) or until a cube of day-old bread browns in 40 seconds. Fry cannelloni, 4 at a time, for 2-3 minutes until crisp and golden. Drain on absorbent kitchen paper. Keep hot until all the cannelloni are cooked. Serve, garnished with lemon slices and parsley.

Serves 4.

CRISPY NOODLES

- 185 g (6 oz/1⅔ cups) short cut noodles
- 1 large Spanish onion, thinly sliced
- 155 ml (5 fl oz/⅔ cup) milk
- 2 tablespoons plain flour
- vegetable oil for deep frying
- salt
- spring onion tassels and lemon butterflies, to garnish

In a large saucepan of boiling salted water, cook the noodles until just tender. Drain, rinse in cold water, then drain again thoroughly.

In a deep fat fryer, heat oil to 190C (375F) or until a cube of day-old bread browns in 40 seconds. Fry noodles in 4 batches until crisp and golden. Drain on absorbent kitchen paper. Keep hot.

Separate onion slices into rings. Dip onion rings in milk, then toss in flour. Fry in 2 batches, in the same way as noodles, until crisp and golden. Mix with noodles and sprinkle with salt. Serve, with each portion garnished with a spring onion tassel and lemon butterfly.

Serves 4 as an accompaniment to fried or grilled meat or fish.

NOODLE PANCAKES

- 30 g (1 oz) noodles
- 60 g (2 oz) ham
- 2 eggs, beaten
- 1 tablespoon chopped fresh parsley
- 1 tablespoon grated Parmesan cheese
- salt and pepper
- vegetable oil for frying
- lemon slices and sprigs of parsley, to garnish

In a large saucepan of boiling salted water, cook the noodles until just tender. Drain. Chop noodles and ham. In a bowl, mix with eggs, parsley and Parmesan cheese. Season to taste with salt and pepper.

In a frying pan, heat oil. Drop tablespoons of noodle mixture into pan. Cook until underside is crisp and brown, then turn over and fry other side.

Remove from pan. Drain on absorbent kitchen paper. Serve at once, garnished with lemon slices and sprigs of parsley.

Serves 4.

CHOCOLATE & NUT BOWS

- 30 g (1 oz/¼ cup) blanched almonds
- 30 g (1 oz/¼ cup) hazelnuts
- 250 g (8 oz/4 cups) pasta bows
- 30 g (1 oz/6 teaspoons) butter
- 60 g (2 oz/½ cup) plain (dark) chocolate, coarsely chopped
- 30 g (1 oz/6 teaspoons) demerara sugar

Put nuts in a grill pan under a medium grill. Cook, stirring frequently, until golden brown. Chop nuts coarsely.

In a large saucepan of boiling salted water, cook pasta bows until tender.

Drain pasta and put into a warmed serving dish. Stir in butter. Add nuts, chocolate and demerara sugar. Toss to mix. Serve at once.

Serves 4.

Variations: Use pasta butterflies instead of bows, if preferred.

ALMOND RAVIOLI

- 125 g (4 oz/1¼ cups) ground almonds
- 125 g (4 oz/½ cup) caster sugar
- 2 egg yolks
- 30 g (1 oz/6 teaspoons) butter
- 1 quantity Pasta Dough
- Greek style yogurt and raspberry leaves, to decorate

RASPBERRY SAUCE:

- 500 g (1 lb) raspberries
- 125 g (4 oz/½ cup) caster sugar

To make sauce, reserve a few raspberries for decoration and put raspberries and sugar into a saucepan. Heat gently until juice begins to run. Press through a sieve and set aside.

In a bowl, mix together ground almonds, sugar and egg yolks. In a small saucepan, melt butter. Add to almond mixture. Roll out pasta dough, see page 10. Make ravioli, see page 12, filling with the ground almond paste.

In a large saucepan of boiling salted water, cook ravioli for about 10 minutes. Drain. Meanwhile, in a saucepan, heat raspberry sauce. Pour a pool of sauce onto each plate and arrange ravioli on top. Pipe a circle of yogurt around dish then, using a skewer make a web effect. Decorate with reserved raspberries and raspberry leaves.

Serves 4.

APPLE LASAGNE

875 g (1¾ lb) cooking apples
30 g (1 oz/6 teaspoons) butter
60 g (2 oz/¼ cup) caster sugar
30 g (1 oz/¼ cup) raisins
¼ teaspoon mixed spice
6 sheets lasagne
30 g (1 oz/¼ cup) finely chopped walnuts
whipped cream, to serve
CUSTARD:
315 ml (10 fl oz/1¼ cups) milk
1 egg, plus 1 egg yolk
3 teaspoons cornflour
3 teaspoons caster sugar
icing sugar for sprinkling

To make custard, in a saucepan, heat milk. In a bowl, mix together egg, egg yolk, cornflour and sugar. Pour hot milk onto egg mixture. Stir, return to saucepan and heat gently until thickened. Set aside.

Peel, core and slice apples. Put in a saucepan with butter, sugar and a little water. Cook for 10 minutes, or until soft. Stir in raisins and mixed spice.

Preheat oven to 190C (375F/Gas 5). Butter an ovenproof dish.

Meanwhile, in a large pan of boiling water, cook lasagne. Drain. Layer lasagne and apple mixture in the dish, ending with a layer of apple. Pour custard over apple. Sprinkle with walnuts. Bake in oven for 25 minutes. Sprinkle with icing sugar and serve with cream.

Serves 4.

INDIAN MILK PUDDING

30 g (1 oz/6 teaspoons) butter
60 g (2 oz) spaghetti, broken into 2.5 cm (1 in) pieces
940 ml (30 fl oz/3¾ cups) milk
4 cardamon pods, crushed
6 teaspoons sultanas
30 g (1 oz/¼ cup) flaked almonds
60 g (2 oz/¼ cup) caster sugar
silver leaf, to decorate, if desired

In a heavy saucepan, melt butter. Add spaghetti and cook, stirring, until spaghetti begins to brown.

Add milk, cardamon pods, sultanas and almonds. Simmer briskly for about 20 minutes, stirring frequently. Add sugar and cook for 5 more minutes.

Leave to cool, stirring occasionally. Pour into a serving dish, cover and refrigerate overnight. Serve cold, decorated with silver leaf.

Serves 4.

POLISH NOODLES

- 250 g (8 oz) tagliatelle
- 9 teaspoons poppy seeds
- 30 g (1 oz/6 teaspoons) butter
- 6 teaspoons clear honey
- 60 g (2 oz/⅓ cup) glacé cherries, chopped
- 30 g (1 oz/2 tablespoons) chopped mixed citrus peel
- glacé cherries and strips of angelica, to decorate

In a large saucepan of boiling water, cook tagliatelle until tender. Drain.

Meanwhile, put poppy seeds in a frying pan. Cook poppy seeds over a medium heat for 1 minute, shaking.

In a saucepan, melt butter. Add honey, cherries and mixed citrus peel. Put tagliatelle in a warmed serving dish. Pour over honey mixture. Mix well. Sprinkle poppy seeds over top. Decorate with glacé cherries and angelica.

Serves 4.

APRICOT WALNUT LAYER

- 125 g (4 oz/1 cup) dried apricots, soaked overnight
- 2.5 cm (1 in) piece of cinnamon stick
- juice and finely grated peel 1 orange
- 90 g (3 oz/½ cup) brown sugar
- 2 teaspoons arrowroot
- 30 g (1 oz/½ cup) fine fresh breadcrumbs
- 125 g (4 oz) tagliatelle
- 60 g (2 oz/½ cup) ground walnuts
- 30 g (1 oz/6 teaspoons) butter
- walnut halves and apricot pieces, to decorate
- whipped cream flavoured with grated orange peel, to serve

Drain apricots, reserving juice. Put apricots, 6 teaspoons of juice, cinnamon, orange juice and peel and 30 g (1 oz/2 tablespoons) sugar into a saucepan. Bring to the boil, then cover and simmer for 10-15 minutes until tender.

Blend arrowroot with a little water. Add to apricots. Cook gently, stirring, until mixture has thickened. Leave to cool.

Preheat oven to 190C (375F/Gas 5). Butter a soufflé dish, then coat with breadcrumbs.

Meanwhile, in a large saucepan of boiling salted water, cook tagliatelle until tender. Drain.

Put one-third of the pasta in dish. Cover with apricot mixture. Cover with half remaining pasta. Mix walnuts and remaining sugar together, spread over pasta. Top with final layer of pasta.

In a saucepan, melt butter. Pour over pasta. Bake in the oven for 25 minutes. Turn out onto a serving dish. Decorate with walnut halves and apricot pieces and serve with flavoured cream.

Serves 4-6.

DATE & NOODLE PUDDING

250 g (8 oz) tagliatelle	
155 ml (5 fl oz/⅔ cup) Greek strained yogurt	
125 g (4 oz/½ cup) mascarpone	
1 teaspoon cornflour	
3 eggs, beaten	
6 teaspoons clear honey	
1 teaspoon ground cinnamon	
60 g (2 oz/⅓ cup) chopped dates	
60 g (2 oz/⅓ cup) sultanas	
60 g (2 oz/⅓ cup) glacé cherries, chopped	
whipped cream, glacé cherries and strips of angelica, to decorate	

In a large saucepan of boiling salted water, cook tagliatelle until tender. Drain.

Preheat oven to 180C (350F/Gas 4). Grease a rectangular ovenproof dish. In a bowl, mix yogurt and mascarpone. Stir in cornflour, eggs, honey, cinnamon, dates, sultanas and cherries.

Add tagliatelle and stir well to distribute fruit evenly. Spoon into the dish and level the surface.

Bake in the oven for about 40 minutes until set and golden brown. Serve warm or cold, cut into slices; decorate with whipped cream, glacé cherries and angelica.

Serves 4.

PEAR & PASTA PUDDING

90 g (3 oz/⅔ cup) macaroni	
500 ml (16 fl oz/2 cups) milk	
2 pears	
60 g (2 oz/⅓ cup) raisins	
finely grated peel of 1 lemon	
½ teaspoon ground cinnamon	
3 teaspoons light soft brown sugar	
1 egg, separated	
30 g (1 oz/6 teaspoons) butter	
bay leaf, to decorate	

Preheat oven to 180C (350F/Gas 4). Grease an ovenproof dish. Put macaroni and milk into a saucepan. Bring to the boil, then simmer for 10 minutes. Remove from heat.

Peel and core one pear. Chop roughly and add to macaroni with raisins, lemon peel, cinnamon, sugar and egg yolk. In a bowl, whisk egg white until stiff. Gently fold into macaroni mixture, then pour into the dish. Bake in the oven for 30 minutes.

Peel and core remaining pear. Cut into slices lengthwise. Arrange decoratively on top of the pudding. In a saucepan, melt butter. Brush over pears. Return to the oven for 10 minutes until pear slices are brown. Serve, decorated with a bay leaf.

Serves 4.

CHOCOLATE SPAGHETTI

- 60 g (2 oz) plain (dark) chocolate
- 2 eggs
- 220 g (7 oz/$1\frac{3}{4}$ cups) strong plain flour
- chocolate flowers, to decorate

WHITE CHOCOLATE SAUCE:

- 60 g (2 oz) white chocolate
- 155 ml (5 fl oz/$\frac{2}{3}$ cup) double (heavy) cream

Melt chocolate in the top of a double boiler or a bowl set over a saucepan of simmering water. Make pasta, see page 9, adding melted chocolate to egg. Leave to rest for 30 minutes.

Roll out pasta. Roll pasta sheets through the spaghetti cutter. Put a tea towel over the back of a chair. Spread spaghetti out and leave to dry for 30 minutes. In a large saucepan of boiling water, cook spaghetti until tender. Drain.

Meanwhile, make sauce, put white chocolate and cream into a saucepan. Heat gently until melted, then stir until smooth. Drain spaghetti. Serve with sauce, decorated with chocolate flowers.

Serves 4.

MERINGUE PUDDING

- 125 g (4 oz/$\frac{3}{4}$ cup) small pasta shapes
- 440 ml (14 fl oz/$1\frac{3}{4}$ cups) milk
- 90 g (3 oz/$\frac{1}{3}$ cup) caster sugar
- finely grated peel of 1 orange
- 2 eggs, separated
- 30 g (1 oz/6 teaspoons) butter
- kumquat segments and angelica leaves, to decorate

Put pasta shapes and milk into a saucepan. Bring to the boil, then simmer gently for 20 minutes, or until pasta is tender and milk has been absorbed, adding more milk if necessary. Meanwhile, preheat oven to 150C (300F/Gas 2).

Stir 30 g (1 oz/6 teaspoons) sugar into pasta, then stir in orange peel and egg yolks. In a small saucepan, melt butter. Add to pasta mixture. Pour into an ovenproof dish.

In a bowl, whisk egg whites until stiff. Whisk in all but 1 teaspoon of remaining sugar. Spoon or pipe over pasta mixture. Sprinkle with remaining sugar. Bake in the oven for 30 minutes, or until golden brown and crisp. Serve at once, decorated with kumquat segments and angelica leaves.

Serves 4.

INDEX